BATTEN
DOWN THE
HATCHES

PREPARING FOR
THE STORMS OF LIFE

PAT SCOTT

FOREWORD BY DR. PRENTICE A. MEADOR, JR.

LEADER'S GUIDE INCLUDED

NASHVILLE, TENNESSEE

To Bob,

my faithful companion for almost thirty-six years.
He was a devoted husband, father, and grandfather.
He loved the Lord, and he loved people.
He made my life unpredictable, interesting, and joyful.

Contents

Foreword

BATTEN DOWN the Hatches was not written in the sterile atmosphere of a library, but in the storm following the horror of a murder.

In one of our nation's most famous driveway shootings, a gunman ended Bob Scott's life. From the *New York Times* to the *San Francisco Chronicle,* the media recounted the events of Bob's murder. Pat, his dear wife of many years, witnessed the moment of terror.

There followed a funeral, the loving support of Christian and non-Christian friends, a murder trial, and a remarkable story of a woman living through one of the most dangerous storms of life.

This is uniquely Pat Scott's story. No one else can tell it.

You will not only appreciate reading this compelling book because it was born out of adversity, but because you will also face your own storms of life. If you're like me, you need help anywhere you can get it, especially from those who have already experienced the storms. In that way, this book has credibility, authority, and a spiritual dimension that marks it as a powerful, practical story.

I know Pat Scott well. I held her hand through some of the traumatic events following Bob's murder. I have watched her walk down the path of joy, rather than bitterness. She has not lost her zest for life nor her sense of humor. She has reached out to others in grief through grief recovery groups held in her own home. Stability, peace of mind, forgiveness of the murderer, and joy—these distinctive benchmarks have given her a new ministry to people. Murder did not fracture her hope. She has learned to sail through one of the fiercest storms of life. That's a good reason to read *Batten Down the Hatches.*

PRENTICE A. MEADOR, JR., Ph.D.
Minister

Acknowledgments

THE LORD has provided so much of what I needed to write this book: hope for the future, the beautiful surroundings of my mountain retreat in New Mexico, and precious friends and family who have supported and encouraged me.

My daughter, Michelle Tucker, and her husband, Randy, deserve more thanks than I can possibly give. They taught me to use the computer and helped me over countless obstacles in this effort.

Dr. Tim Young is the person who deserves the credit for causing me to focus on the fact that certain traits must have already been in place before my tragedy.

I also thank Flossye Gagneux and Ron Verner for their time spent in reading this manuscript and in supporting my efforts.

Preface

PEOPLE STILL REMEMBER the headlines and ask about the tragedy that struck our family. I believe that what people really want to know is this: "How have you managed to cope with the experience of having a gun held in your face or the horror of seeing your husband shot in the head? How could you endure that lengthy police investigation—being the focus of relentless media coverage? How could you survive a whole year of preparation for a murder trial and then sit in the courtroom face to face with your attacker day after day?" Most people wonder whether I can possibly function as a normal person again. "Are you not a nervous wreck?" they ask. "Don't you have nightmares?"

Scripture clearly assures us that, "In this world you *will* have trouble" (John 16:33). We have been warned—it's up to us to batten down the hatches and make ready for life's storms. We don't know in advance exactly what our troubles will be. As Forest Gump's mama put it, "Life is like a box of chocolates; you never know what you're gonna get." But I like what Charlie Brown once said: "Life is like an ice cream cone—you gotta lick it!" I'm convinced that if we're going to lick it, we must start getting ready well *before* the stormy winds send us reeling.

As hurricane Andrew boiled its way toward the Florida coast in 1992, residents began to get ready for the onslaught of that violent storm. They nailed boards over doors and windows. They brought outdoor furniture and plants inside. They stored extra food and water. Intense preparation was underway well ahead of the storm.

What do you think would have happened if those residents had waited until the violent winds began to rage before making their preparations? They would have found it difficult, if not impossible, to find refuge. The boards would have blown from their hands as they tried to hammer them on the windows. They would have been bombarded with all kinds of flying debris. They might have even died.

That is similar to what happens to people who are in the midst of life's personal storms, if they are unprepared spiritually and emotionally. If you wait until the debris is flying, you will find yourself merely trying to react to the buffeting and never able to feel secure and hopeful. It is sometimes said that there is no way to prepare for some of the harshness that life brings, but I don't believe that. In fact, the premise of this book is that a person can find serenity, security, and strength in times of adversity or disaster when certain traits or attitudes are in place *before* the storm hits.

It reminds me of the man and his son who were driving out to their farm when their car broke down. They decided that they would have to walk the rest of the way. So they took a short-cut across a pasture. Suddenly, they looked back and saw a huge bull running toward them. They began to run, too, but the bull was gaining on them.

Finally the son said, "Dad, perhaps we should just stop and pray."

The father, still running, said, "You can stop if you wish, but I stay prayed up for times like these!"

People who wait until they are in the midst of crisis to begin preparing will probably find the ordeal overpowering. No doubt, you may have already experienced some tragedy or serious loss, whether death, illness, financial reversal, divorce, or some other disappointment. To some extent, we are the sum total of all our life's experiences—the people who have been in our lives, our relationships, the problems that we have encountered, the disasters, the successes, and the failures. These are all things that tend to mold the ways we think and the ways we react to adversity. Indeed, these things will likely determine our responses to problems, unless we make some effort to acquire certain mental, spiritual, and behavioral attitudes. There are some beneficial traits and attitudes that we can acquire in preparation for times of serious adversity.

It will not be the purpose of this writing to tell you that you must respond to tragedy in some specific way. However, there are things that you can do right now to better prepare yourself for future storms. It's only natural that the way our parents responded to difficulties influences the way we respond. But the behavior which comes most naturally is not always the most desirable.

Experts often say that the most important coping skills to possess when the storms of life hit are these:

1. A positive attitude
2. Self-control
3. Self-esteem
4. Extroversion

Before I had read any information about working through adversity, Dr. Tim Young, a family counselor, asked me one night at church what traits had benefited me the most when our tragedy occurred. I carefully thought about that question, and when my list was finished, all four of these traits were on the list. The major difference was that at the top of my list was "the ability to trust God." Notice that these are all areas we can actively work at developing.

Scripture supports the premise that we *can prepare* for the storms of life. The apostle Peter wrote his first letter to Christians dispersed through persecution. The purpose of his letter was to prepare those early Christians for the horrendous suffering he knew they were about to face. Peter obviously believed that some mental preparation could be made for a future time of great hardship.

In 1 Peter 1:13, the apostle wrote to those Christians, saying, "Prepare your minds for action; be self-controlled; set your hope fully on the grace to be given you when Jesus Christ is revealed." Peter was urging them to make themselves ready for some bad things that surely would happen to them. I echo Peter's admonition, because we, too, have been warned that in this world we *will* have trouble. Therefore, our question should not be, "Will we have trouble?" The only question is, "When?" or "How much?" It is up to us to batten down the hatches and prepare for the storms.

PAT SCOTT

"O Death,
where is your victory?"

———

1 CORINTHIANS 15:55

Morning News

xas, Saturday, March 5, 1994   7 Sections   HF   ..   •   25 Cents

'Driveway robbery' shooting victim dies

N. Dallas couple had tried to act cautiously

By Ed Housewright
and Robert Ingrassia
Staff Writers of The Dallas Morning News

Bob and Pat Scott knew to be cautious.

They had just returned to Dallas on Tuesday after two months on South Padre Island but had already heard of "driveway robberies" in and around their Far North Dallas neighborhood, friends said Friday.

So they immediately became concerned when they noticed someone following them as they returned home from dinner and grocery shopping Thursday night.

They waited until the pickup truck was no longer visible before pulling into their driveway in the 5700 block of En'core Drive, a half-mile north of Valley View Center.

■ Safety tips.   26A

Still, they weren't safe.

Mr. Scott, 63, was shot in the head after struggling with a robber and died Friday morning at Parkland Memorial Hospital. Mrs. Scott, 58, was robbed of jewelry at gunpoint but escaped injury.

Friday, friends mourned Mr. Scott, a former bank vice president and founding member of Prestoncrest Church of Christ who took numerous trips with his wife to South Texas and Europe to do church work.

Neighbors and crime watch officials expressed fear and outrage over the shooting. Police, still searching for the killer, vowed

Please see 'DRIVEWAY' on Page 26A.

CHAPTER

1

The Storm

THE NIGHT BREEZE was crisp as the last remnants of winter clung tenaciously to the traditionally mild Texas climate. It was March 3, 1994, and Dallasites were already expecting spring. In fact, I had just set out a few ceramic Easter bunnies before leaving home for an evening of shopping and dinner. My husband Bob and I had dinner at a local Mexican food restaurant before shopping for a few items that we needed for a fish fry, which we were planning a few nights later. Our last stop before returning home was to purchase frames for new pictures of our grandsons.

As we drove toward our home, the traffic was still rather heavy. It was only 8:30 P.M., but at that season of the year darkness had fallen. A maze of headlights danced in our car's rear-view mirror. Bob maneuvered the car into the left-hand lane of traffic and then into the turn lane for our neighborhood. The entrance is a landscaped boulevard accentuated by a brick wall encircling the neighborhood.

Catching me a bit off guard, Bob suddenly asked, "Do you see anyone following us?"

Although we had just returned to Dallas, we had heard a news story about random driveway robberies that had been occurring in the North Dallas area. I glanced over my shoulder toward the busy street from which we had exited. At first I saw nothing, but a second look revealed a two-tone pickup truck stopped in the turn lane. Almost simultaneously my husband was turning into our alley.

I said, "Wait a second—there was a pickup truck."

At that point I could no longer see the turn lane where the pickup truck had been, but I thought that I would be able to see headlights if it really turned into our neighborhood. Seeing no headlights, we proceeded to the back driveway of our home and drove into the garage. I pressed the trunk release button before hopping out of the car and giving my handbag a toss toward the locked door leading into the house.

As I turned around, I saw a young black man slither into the garage on my side of the car. He held his head down, not looking at me, as he approached. It was almost as if he didn't see me. He was nicely dressed in khaki jeans and a brown leather jacket. Perhaps it was wishful thinking, but for one brief moment I wondered if this could be someone we might know. Suddenly, he faced me squarely, and my eyes fastened upon a deadly-looking gun in his right hand. I screamed in terror as he grabbed me around the neck and thrust the weapon against my temple.

Bob was on the opposite side of the car and had been taking packages from the back seat before my chilling scream. Now I could not see him at all as my attacker had pinned me against the side of the car. The young man was considerably taller than I and had a rather athletic build. He resolutely kept that gun pointed at my left temple, and as I glanced left, I found myself looking straight into the eerie blackness of that gun barrel. It was like hanging on a precipice between life and death.

"Give me them rings!" he gruffly muttered.

Suddenly I became aware that he was trying to force the rings off my left hand. The rings were not budging, but the skin was!

I quickly said, "Wait! I'll give you the rings!"

As I began removing the rings, I heard Bob run into the alley, yelling, "Help! Help!" I froze for a moment, fearing how my attacker might react. Surprisingly, he paid no attention to Bob's actions. He continued collecting my rings.

> *One loud cracking sound shattered the silence of that spring night and the tranquillity of my life.*

One ring slipped from my hand and rolled under the car, but he didn't hear it because the garage was carpeted. Then he pushed me in front of him out of the garage and into the alley. Bob was standing there. No help had come.

The gunman noticed that I was wearing a watch. "Give me that watch," he demanded. The watch was nothing special, but as I began removing it I remembered that an expensive bracelet was on the other arm. Fortunately, he had not noticed it.

"Where's your purse?" he yelled at me. At that point I had no idea where it was and muttered something to that affect.

The attacker released me and began walking toward Bob. "Give him what he wants, Bob," I said to my husband.

Bob slowly began removing his watch and rings.

"Give me your wallet!" shouted the gunman. But suddenly the clip somehow fell from his gun, spilling bullets all over the alley. Our attacker raced over and picked up the clip and some of the bullets. It has been said that he probably had only one bullet left in the gun after the clip had fallen. As if in anger and frustration, the gunman rushed toward Bob.

"Oh, Lord, please don't let this happen," I whispered. One loud cracking sound shattered the silence of that spring night and the tranquillity of my life.

Bob's body fell to the ground like metal to a magnet. I stood frozen for one awful moment, not even wondering whether the man might shoot me, too. The gunman turned and ran away on foot down the alley. There was no other person or vehicle in view, but his driver had probably waited near the entrance of our neighborhood.

I raced in the opposite direction to my neighbor's home and banged frantically on the door. "Help! Help!" I screamed.

As my neighbor opened her door, I shouted, "Please call 9-1-1. Bob's been shot!"

Quickly, I ran back to my husband's crumpled body, lying face down in the alley. Kneeling over him I said, "Bob, Bob, can you hear me?"

He seemed to push up on his hands, lifting his head and shoulders slightly. His breathing made a gurgling sound. Putting my arm around his shoulders, I said, "Just lie still and hang on; help will be here very soon."

Fading Hope

I listened for sirens. There was only silence. It seemed to take forever. At some point I became vaguely aware that there was some man kneeling beside me. Later, I learned that it was one of the neighbors.

I began sliding the palm of my hand over Bob's body trying to find where the bullet had penetrated. Eventually, my hand felt the wound . . . on his forehead! My hope sank.

Car lights were approaching. The car stopped. It was the wife of a pediatrician who lived across the alley from us. We were somewhat blocking her driveway. She ran into her house, bringing back towels for us, and I propped one under Bob's head.

About that time the first police car arrived followed by the ambulance. I felt a small surge of hope. A young police officer pried me away from the scene as the paramedics took charge. The officer began asking me questions, but I could hardly form my words.

Finally, I managed to say, "Please, I want to go in the ambulance with my husband."

"You will go in the ambulance," replied the officer, "but they won't be leaving until they get him stabilized."

"Pat, do you want me to call Michelle?" The voice broke through the melee. It was my neighbor who had called 9-1-1 for me. She had fought her way through a line of police officers to reach me.

"Yes! Yes!" I shouted as the young officer continued trying to question me.

Finally, someone shouted, "Bring her on! We're ready to go!"

As we made our way through the crowd toward the ambulance, I saw Michelle, my daughter, running toward me. We had only a moment to exchange hugs and a few words before I was hustled into the front passenger side of the ambulance. The police officer put his arm around Michelle and began giving her instructions about things that she should do before coming to the hospital. He told her to go home and make arrangements to be at the hospital for quite awhile.

As the ambulance whisked us away, the driver told me to fasten my seat belt. He was traveling very fast with the siren wailing. Each time as he was about to make a sharp turn, he would advise the medics in the back with Bob. Occasionally, I tried to see what was going on in the back but could see very little. I was almost afraid to know. The driver didn't utter a word to me. He seemed to need all his concentration to get us to the hospital. It was fine with me. I was beyond words. I sat silently praying.

I had earlier told the paramedics that our doctors were at Medical City Hospital, but they had replied, "No Ma'am, you need Parkland's Trauma Unit." Parkland Hospital is a large medical study facility and is known for its outstanding trauma unit. It's the hospital to which President John F. Kennedy was taken when he was shot in the head.

As the ambulance pulled into Parkland Emergency and stopped, the paramedics were out the back door and quickly wheeling Bob away. I started to follow, but someone directed me another way. Inside, they only took my name before escorting me through security and then to a small private room somewhere in the emergency area.

Shock and Support

"Would you like to see a chaplain?" asked some of the staff.

"No, I think I'd like to just sit quietly for a moment," I replied.

I dropped into a chair and sat there in stunned, senseless silence. *What has happened to us?* I thought as I looked down at my hands. They were bloody, and blood was under my fingernails. I don't know how long I sat there alone, but it didn't seem long at all.

Suddenly, the door opened and standing there was a close friend who had been a former minister at our church. With him was his wife and another precious couple who were wonderful friends. Their faces were truly welcome sights. A short time later, Michelle and her husband, Randy, arrived. She had already called our son in Louisville, Kentucky, and she had also made arrangements for someone to care for her two small boys.

The attending physician entered the room. He was very kind and gentle.

"It doesn't look good," he said. "We will know more after the brain scan."

Finally, the doctor told me that Michelle and I could go in to see Bob. I suppose there's no way that I could have been prepared for what I was about to see. Bob's head was swollen to the point of being unrecognizable. Bandages covered the wound, and gauze was wrapped around his head. His eyes were closed but looked purple . . . probably because of blood. He was swathed in tubing performing various bodily tasks. He was a complete stranger. Shock swept over me. I felt weak, and I just stood there frozen. Michelle took hold of Bob's hand and stood quietly. There was no response from him at all. We didn't stay very long, because I felt too weak to stand.

As we left that room, everyone was offering to get water for me. Seeing my ashen face, they were certain that I was about to faint. Dazed, I sat back down in my chair. People kept offering to do something for me, but this time nothing could be done by human hands.

The Trauma Unit at Parkland Hospital has very tight security, and no one is allowed in without a pass. With that fact in mind, you cannot possibly fathom the overwhelming number of caring friends who began appearing there as the anxious moments ticked by. The hospital was so kind to accommodate the wishes of our friends to be there with us. The elders from the church were there, and periodically throughout the

> *Periodically throughout the night everyone gathered together to pray. We all knew that the outcome of all this was in God's hands.*

night everyone gathered together to pray. We all knew that the outcome of all this was in God's hands. No matter what happened, God was right there with us. He would give us strength for what must be endured.

Many of the men standing there were close friends of Bob's. They had played golf together or gone on hunting trips together. One couple arrived sometime after midnight, having driven in from out of town after hearing of the shooting. It was a couple with whom we had spent many happy times traveling. My sisters and their husbands arrived and made their way through the crowd. Each time I tried to recount what had happened to us, the details sounded so senseless, and I could hardly make complete sentences.

All Through the Night

The police detective in charge of investigating this case arrived and asked to talk with me privately. Somehow we did find a spot away from the crowd. He asked for more details about how this attack had happened. He wanted a description of the attacker. It was very difficult to make my mind function well enough to make sense, but I tried hard to help the detective.

Sometime later I became more conscious that my hands were still bloody and that blood was still caked under my fingernails. I decided that I should wash my hands, and yet I felt some kind of strange reluctance to do so. I made my way to the wash room, turned on the warm water, and watched as my husband's blood swept from my fingers down the drain.

The doctors made frequent trips from ICU to talk with me during the night and early morning hours. The large crowd was still there, and some had devised pallets on the floor. Finally, the doctors made that dreaded visit. This time they had to ask me that tough question that doctors must sometimes ask the family of a patient who is on life support.

"Mrs. Scott, it may be that at some point the decision will have to be made by *you* to remove life support. Can you make that decision?"

I had already heard the hopeless prognosis and had seen Bob's condition. I knew very well what Bob's own decision would be. When one has a strong belief that heaven awaits when physical life ends, such decisions can be made with a bit more confidence, especially when a person's meaningful life on this earth is clearly over.

And so I replied, "I believe that I will be able to make that decision."

The doctor looked at me with a kind and steady gaze and said, "I am so glad to hear you say that. So many folks have great difficulty trying to make that decision."

I made my way back into the crowded room where I had been sitting but suddenly realized that I felt faint. I needed more air or a cooler place. Someone took me down the hall to an empty surgery waiting room and brought me a fresh coke with ice in it. Soon I was feeling better.

As Dawn Came

As dawn neared, I noticed that some of the people had found the cafeteria and were munching pastries and drinking coffee. They were offering to bring me food, but eating was out of the question. Calls were coming in constantly, and one of the church secretaries was handling the calls. The press was down-stairs, requesting interviews. They would not be allowed on the trauma floor unless I approved. That was welcome news, because I certainly wasn't ready for the press. At almost any other hospital I would not have been protected from the press.

As morning came, more friends and relatives arrived. Bob's brother and his wife had driven all night to be there after receiving the shocking news about ten o'clock the night before.

Then, our son Keith arrived from Louisville, Kentucky. He had been unable to get a flight until morning. He had spent a devastating night all alone after receiving the shattering news. We warmly embraced.

"It's almost over for Dad," I said.

The doctor had told me that I would not have to make the decision about removing life support, because Bob's body was shutting down on its own. The doctor said that we could go in to be with Bob as his heart began to stop. So, five or six of us went inside. We couldn't even hold his hands, because police detectives had ordered his hands put into paper bags in order to preserve evidence. In fact, there was almost no place to lay a hand on him because of the wires and tubing.

> *"You have been a good daddy. Just go and be with Jesus. It's okay."*

Michelle whispered, "You have been a good daddy. Just go and be with Jesus. It's okay."

I found a bare spot on his shoulder and kissed it. I glanced at the machine monitoring the heart rate. The lines became flatter, and then it was over. The nurse turned everything off. We all stood silently for moment, and then the nurse began to explain some formalities that would have to be handled before leaving the hospital.

We all walked slowly out of ICU and down the corridor toward the large crowd of waiting friends and relatives. We gathered once again for prayer. Gradually people began leaving, but some of the hospital staff instructed me and my family that, if we hoped to avoid the press, we should leave through a special exit.

It felt strange to walk out into the glare of the morning sun. It was about 11:30 A.M. when I climbed into the car with my two children and son-in-law for the ride to Michelle and Randy's home. We had already been advised not to go to my home because reporters were waiting there. The police had spent the night there conducting their investigation and gathering evidence.

The Media Mania

As I walked into Michelle's home, the television was on. It was so ironic that the noon news should be on right at that moment. Somehow they had already gotten pictures of Bob and me, and they were doing a lengthy coverage of the "driveway robbery and murder" which had occurred during the night. It had never occurred to me to imagine what it would be like to be the central figure in such a story, and even then, it did not feel real.

Randy's family had taken our young grandsons home with them. Painfully, I began to realize what a great loss this would be to our three-and-one-half-year-old Scotty. He and his "Dado" (the name he had devised for Bob) were very close buddies. Scotty would have to try to understand that he would never see his "Dado" again.

Soon the house was busy with people coming and going and the telephone ringing. People were urging me to rest or eat, but neither was in the realm of possibility for me. I was still wearing the same jeans and shirt that I had been wearing on Thursday evening when we were attacked. It was a very strange phenomena, but I didn't want to get cleaned up. I received many visitors in that same disheveled condition. Shock can do strange things. On the surface I was calm and composed and talked freely with all who came.

It was probably 11:00 P.M. before I was able to force myself to bathe and get ready for bed. It had been thirty-nine hours since I had slept. Michelle, who is a take-charge person, had called a doctor, and medication was administered before I finally went to bed. I fell into a deep sleep and slept soundly all night. I awoke the next morning feeling rested. Surprisingly, I awoke feeling peaceful—not that sickening horror that might be expected when waking anew to the grim reality of what had happened. My mind felt clear, almost as if I had remained gently aware of the tragedy even while sleeping. For the first time in my life, I was experiencing how mightily God can protect and comfort His own people through an unthinkable ordeal.

For the first time in my life, I was experiencing how mightily God can protect and comfort His own people through an unthinkable ordeal.

The days to follow were not what most families commonly experience as they prepare for the funeral of a loved one. There was no time to quietly grieve and make preparations. One of the first calls on Saturday morning was from the police detective on our case. He wanted to take me downtown to try to do a composite sketch of our attacker. I told him that we needed a few hours to finalize funeral arrangements, and he reminded me that the press would be hawking my every move.

He was right. The media circus had begun! Within a few hours my private life had become public, and our story was on the front pages of newspapers everywhere, and our pictures were on every television channel. Reporters were clamoring for the story.

It was obvious that I couldn't go to my house. It was finally decided that my son and son-in-law would go there in order to get burial clothing for Bob. Just as we had been warned, the cameras were there and rolling. Keith and Randy found our back driveway cordoned off by yellow crime-scene tape, which had been placed there by the police. They insisted to the reporters that the family would have no comment and finally were able to complete their mission.

We actually got to make a trip to the funeral home briefly to take care of a few simple formalities. Most of our arrangements had been pre-arranged. The decision about opening the casket had to be made, and we felt it should be closed. Even at the funeral home we were vulnerable to prying reporters.

> *A major aspect of God's comfort in tragedy seems to be the service rendered by His people.*

People from the church supported us by taking care of our every need. Every meal was not only prepared for us but served. A major aspect of God's comfort in tragedy seems to be the service rendered by His people. Before the detective came to take me to the police station, we had a quick lunch.

Picturing the Killer

Keith accompanied me on the trip downtown. The part of the police station where composite pictures are sketched looks like a warehouse. Every sound reverberated as I climbed the staircase to the second floor. Keith had to wait downstairs because they wanted my clearest memory recall. The police artist sat at a desk surrounded by "mug" books. He carefully began explaining how the process would work.

"We will concentrate on one feature at a time. First, I need for you to look at some of these pictures and see if you can find a face shape that resembles your attacker."

I was not sure that I could identify or reproduce the face of the attacker, because he had tried to avoid allowing me to see his face.

"I believe his face was shaped somewhat like this one," I said, pointing to a rather oval-shaped face.

The artist sketched the shape of the face on his pad.

"Now what about his hair?" he asked.

"Very closely cut," I replied.

"Any distinct sectioning?" he asked.

I wasn't sure about that, so he moved on.

"Let's look at eyes now," he said, motioning to another book. We went through the same procedure on every feature—nose, mouth, ears. Finally, we had a picture.

"What do you think?" he asked, studying my expression.

"Well, it's probably as close as I can get," I replied.

I was wondering how often these composite sketches had proven to look enough like the criminal to be helpful in making an arrest, so I asked the question.

The artist said, "Oh, it goes both ways. Sometimes they are pretty good likenesses. At other times they turn out not to be at all similar. There are so many factors involved, not the least of which is the trauma of the victim who is attempting to recall a horror. Sometimes the human mind blocks it so completely that we try hypnotism, but I don't believe that you are in that much shock."

"Well, I don't know about that," I said. Yet, my mind did seem surprisingly clear and alert. On the way home, our detective told us that the composite would be put in the newspaper next week.

Our Church Family

The next day was Sunday, and Keith and I decided to attend early worship services. We intentionally slipped in a few minutes after services had begun. We made our way into a pew and suddenly realized that the person on my right was a female police officer from the District Attorney's office. She had already called Michelle's home to offer her services if protection was needed. I had not yet responded to her kind offer. How providential that I should sit right beside her.

The sermon and the announcements were filled with references to what had happened to our family. This church had been a major part of our lives for a long time. Bob and I had helped to begin it in 1971, and Bob had been one of its first elders. Our children had grown up there. These people were family to us, and they were grieving Bob's death just as we were. As the service began to draw to a close, I wrote a little note to the young police officer sitting next to me thanking her for her call and assuring her that we would be in touch. Then Keith and I made our way to the exit before the service ended. There were one or two people in the foyer but no recognizable press.

The afternoon was busy, filled with lots of friends and family. We also had meetings with the ministers who would be conducting the funeral service. We were receiving word that friends from Nebraska, Illinois, New Mexico, Kentucky, Oklahoma, and California were enroute to be present for the memorial service on Monday. We felt very warmed with the knowledge that so many people cared so much.

I also became increasingly aware that many of these people were feeling their own personal sense of loss and despair. Bob had touched many lives in special ways. He had taught Bible class for newly married couples and had worked with young singles. There were men with whom he had served as an elder and men with whom he had golfed, fished, worked, and traveled. I allowed myself to bask in the warmth of the love that was being poured out upon our family, because I firmly believed it to be a gift from God.

Celebrating Bob's Victory

By the time Monday, March 7, 1994, came, all plans were in place. There would be no casket at the front of the large church auditorium. My children and I had decided that this would be a memorial service, honoring Bob's life and celebrating his victory in Jesus. Bob had spent much of his life in preparation for the time when he would depart this physical existence. It would really be incongruous for this service to be one of deep gloom, and so we would view this occasion more from Bob's perspective than from our own deepest yearnings to have him back with us. How could we wish him back from his glorious reward?

> *I allowed myself to bask in the warmth of the love that was being poured out upon our family, because I firmly believed it to be a gift from God.*

We also chose not to have a funeral limousine come for us. We would travel to the church in the same dark blue Cadillac that Bob and I were driving on the night of his death. We drove to the north portico of the building which would allow us to enter unnoticed by the press. A little shock swept over us as we drove up to see the parking lot overflowing with traffic and cars parked on the shoulders of the road as far as we could see.

As our procession started down the aisle, the audience rose. There were easily more than a thousand people present. The cameras of the press were rolling discreetly from a glassed-in room at the rear of the sanctuary. As Keith escorted me down the aisle, my mind slipped back to 1984 when he had escorted me down this same aisle at Michelle's wedding.

The singing of the chorus was movingly beautiful as they sang joyous music. Their voices were heard that evening on the NBC national news coverage of the memorial service for the "Victim of Dallas' Driveway Robbery Spree." The minister opened the service with the scripture, "O Death, where *is* your victory?" The newspaper printed the next morning much of what he said.

Then the former minister and longtime friend who had been at the hospital with me on Thursday night and Friday morning reflected on memories of Bob's life and even related a few humorous stories. The newspaper also printed some of his comments. In en-

> *"The man who pulled the trigger that night really just blasted open the gates of heaven for Bob."*

larged print for emphasis, the newspaper quoted this minister's statement: "The man who pulled the trigger that night really just blasted open the gates of heaven for Bob."

As our family sat there on the front row, I glanced over at our little Scotty—Bob's pride and joy. Scotty had flown with some of our friends to South Padre Island only a couple of weeks earlier to visit us. Bob had taken him out for a boat ride, and we had fed the sea gulls and hunted sea shells on the beach. Little had we suspected that those good times would be our last together. Now, Scotty was sitting very still and quiet on his dad's lap, and his big blue eyes were fixed on the speaker as if trying to make some sense of all this.

Beginning of the Aftermath

During the weeks that followed, there was not only media coverage, but police investigators and detectives were constantly in and out, trying to resolve the case and make an arrest. Only a few days after our tragedy, a second driveway murder was committed, which brought even more media hype. The wire services had latched onto the stories, and these two cases were quickly dubbed "the driveway murders" by the press.

Even national programs, such as *American Journal,* were trying to persuade me to be on their programs. I always declined, but some of them did the story anyway. I'm sure that everyone who suddenly finds themselves in the glare of the public eye goes through the same kind of disbelief and dismay. I kept trying to understand why this had become a national story. People are murdered in cities across this country every day. The headlines screamed to the world that crime and violence were out of control. The stories seemed to say, "If this can happen to Bob and Pat Scott, it can happen to you."

> *Still, we knew that we were safe in the arms of God.*

The people of Dallas were frozen with fear. New security lights were going up all over the neighborhoods, special meetings were being held, and gated communities became big sellers.

For our family, being in the center of such widespread trepidation was like being in the middle of a tremendous storm for which we were somehow responsible. We were attempting to cope with our own personal loss, but simultaneously we were being buffeted by the fear and insecurity of an entire community. Still, we knew that we were safe in the arms of God.

*"Forgetting what is behind
and straining toward what is ahead,
I press on toward the goal
to win the prize for which
God has called me heavenward
in Christ Jesus."*

<small>PHILIPPIANS 3:13</small>

N. Dallas man shot in robbery

Incident follows 3 arrests in 'driveway' crimes

By Dan R. Barber
and Nora Lopez
Staff Writers of The Dallas Morning News

A Far North Dallas man was shot and critically wounded Thursday night in what police said appeared to be the latest and most brutal in a series of "driveway robberies."

Bob Scott, 63, of the 5700 block of En'core Drive, remained in critical condition at Parkland Memorial Hospital early Friday with a single gunshot wound in the head.

The shooting occurred a day after police arrested three men suspected of committing most of two dozen similar robberies, many of them in the same general area, since early January.

Mrs. Scott was at the hospital with her husband late Thursday night and unavailable for comment. Police had not yet interviewed her, Detective Bricker said.

"They pulled into the driveway, the suspect ran into the garage (and) confronted the wife at gunpoint. Her husband came to her aid, there was a struggle on the driveway (and) the husband was shot in the alley."

— Detective Bill Bricker

Reprinted with Permission of *The Dallas Morning News*.

2

Changes in
Our Course
Are Certain

IN MOST normal grief and loss situations, the survivors begin to experience a quiet period in the days and weeks which follow the funeral of a loved one. Relatives and friends usually leave and resume their day-to-day activities. The reality and finality of the situation begin to be absorbed during that time. It's then that most families write notes of appreciation to those who have comforted them, and they start the adjustment process. But the Scott family was deprived of such a quiet post-funeral period.

Finally, I was allowed to return to my home. It felt good to be in the familiar surroundings. Just to walk into my own kitchen gave me a sense of connection with a former time. Surprisingly, I felt no anxiety about the violence that had happened at this place. Still, things were very different, and being at home seemed to shine a spotlight on the fact that Bob was *not* there. It forced me to acknowledge that my life had forever changed.

There is something about the grief and loss process that affects the human body as an illness. I felt as if I were trying to recover from a serious surgery, and perhaps the surgeon had forgotten to suture the wound. My energy level was far from normal. I was never able to go to bed early, because so much was happening. Each night when I fell into bed, I slept the sleep of total exhaustion.

Many people tell me that they are unable to sleep when they have experienced traumatic events. But I slept a deep and dreamless sleep without medication every night. The only night that I was ever given medication was the night after the robbery and shooting. I have wondered at times about that dreamless sleep but have decided that it is yet another gift from God.

The magnitude of the changes going on in my life at that time were enough to keep me constantly reeling. The second driveway murder brought the press back to my door, and once again the television screen flashed our pictures and the bloody scene in our alley.

> *It's change for better that most of us believe we can handle—like suddenly inheriting several million dollars.*

The police were in hot pursuit of those who killed my husband. Various detectives and police officers trailed in and out of my home almost constantly, going over the sequence of events that had occurred on March third. Numerous times I walked them through the scenario of the robbery in our garage, driveway, and alley. For days they searched for the spent bullet. I made trips downtown to the jail to view lineups. Some evenings they brought pictures for me to try to identify.

Then, the police chief decided to put a new lead detective on the case. And once again I spent many hours going over every detail of what had happened. However, the new detective was very experienced, and I felt renewed hope that our attacker would be apprehended. This detective was not only smart, he also didn't seem to sleep. He was literally working night and day. In police jargon, this was a "high profile" case, and the pressure weighed heavily on everyone involved.

For Better or For Worse

It's not uncommon that major changes come into the lives of people. It happens quite regularly and is a part of life. My experience was unique only in that I was not coping with one major change but a whole array of major changes. I had lost my mate of thirty-six years, my private life was suddenly public, I was thrown into a huge police investigation, and my own life was being threatened to the point of requiring police protection.

Change is a built-in ingredient of this life's sojourn. Like death, it's a certainty, but change comes in many forms. Some are changes for better, and some are changes for worse. There are changes that we can *expect,* and changes that we *never* could have foreseen.

It's change for better that most of us believe we can handle—like suddenly inheriting several million dollars. Most of us feel we could make *that* adjustment. (Although, truthfully, it might surprise us to learn some of the complications involved with such an inheritance.)

Change for worse is the kind of change that's dreaded—loss of a job, serious illness, broken families, death, etc. People will often refuse to even contemplate the possibility of such changes in their lives, and they certainly cannot bear to make preparations for such things.

Some changes are predictable. We often think that these expected changes can be handled—changes such as the arrival of a new baby, your children reaching the teenage years, or the aging process. Yet, strangely enough, even these predictable changes seem to be tough to handle.

It is understandable that sudden and unexpected changes might cause difficult adjustments, but, for certain people, *any* change causes unusual discomfort. Just as optimism is a difficult trait for some people to acquire, the ability to accept change can be an extraordinary struggle for some.

My younger child disliked *any change* so much that each year when summer came, it took weeks to convince him to switch into short pants, and he always wanted to be in his own bed at night, no matter where we were. I can hardly believe that today he's the one who lives so far away from home.

Resisting Change

Human nature tends to resist change. We get comfortable with the way things are, and it takes energy to do things in new ways. We are much more comfortable with what is familiar.

I remember when NASA was conducting the first space shots. There was an amusing story about a little 85-year-old lady who did not like the thought of rocket ships going into space and said, "They shouldn't be shooting off those rockets; they should stay home and watch TV like God intended."

I chuckled, but when they began putting everything on computers a few years ago, I wanted to join that little woman's club. Only in the last year have I accepted the computer, and that was out of sheer desperation.

Do you remember when AT&T had to split with Southwestern Bell because of monopoly accusations? We had to go out and buy our own telephones. Their rings sounded so strange. Then, the telephone company announced that it would no longer be responsible for the instrument (the telephone itself). The maintenance or repairs were the responsibility of the users. I definitely felt nudged out of my comfort zone and wondered *Why can't things stay the same?*

The fact is, the more unaccepting we are of change, the more stress and anxiety we tend to experience. Inflexible people also tend to experience more conflict. In truth, we might as well assume that life will be filled with changes. We can put that in our computers. Just count on it, especially today, when changes are coming so rapidly. When I was growing up, I don't remember many changes, but today we blink, and everything is new. It's no wonder there is so much stress in our society.

> *Change often brings good things. Even changes that appear to be setbacks often turn out to be blessings.*

Actually, change often brings good things. Even changes that appear to be setbacks often turn out to be blessings. God has a way of bringing success out of failure, good out of evil, and strength out of weakness.

As in all areas of life, you get to choose what your response to change will be. You will likely get to experience a wide variety of changes during your life. So, now is the time to begin *preparing your mind* to expect change and accept it. That trait is called flexibility.

Flexibility

Some people's response to change is to deny it or to scream, cry, and whine about it. Others respond by withdrawing from everyone and everything or even becoming emotionally unstable. Still others play the blame game—blaming everyone, including God. But change is a part of life, and it *will* come.

During the early stages of any major change, especially one that represents a serious loss or setback, any of those responses would be completely normal. However, there comes a time when we must accept the fact that things are going to be different, or things are not going to be what we had always dreamed. People who refuse to face reality become unproductive and lose even more.

The Israelites of the Bible are an example of human refusal to accept a very disappointing change in their tradition. Most of them had always expected a Messiah, and they thought he would be a strong and mighty king, like David, who would set up an earthly kingdom. This had been their dream, but it was not to be! So, they chose a response—*denial*. For many people, denial is the adjustment they make to any change which brings deep disappointment.

> *When you deny unpleasant changes, it causes you to be unproductive, and you lose even more than you have already lost.*

Parents of teenagers suddenly learn that their children are taking drugs. Such behavior is not supposed to happen in their families; therefore, they deny it. A man has a heart attack. That was not in the plan—he denies it. A wife loses her husband. It's too painful to face, so she lives as if he were still there. She is denying reality. When you deny unpleasant changes, it causes you to be unproductive, and you lose even more than you have already lost.

The Israelites, by denying Christ, lost God's promise. The parents of that teenager probably lost their child to drugs. The heart attack victim, by living as if he had no health problem, probably lost his life. The widow lost her usefulness by living a false existence.

Indeed, it's never too early to begin training yourself to be more *flexible,* because there is such a strong likelihood of your having to face numerous changes in your life.

- There will be moves from one city to another, one state to another, or even out of the country.
- People who have been married for quite a number of years without children will, suddenly, *have* children!
- Life-changing health problems can strike at *any* age.
- Standard-of-living changes, either up or down, can be very risky.
- Even the aging process can be very painful when we must watch physical beauty fade, sag, and bulge.
- There are also the changes of empty nest syndrome, aging parents, and loss of loved ones.

The list of potential changes is endless. So, *flexibility* is a necessary survival trait.

When we were touring Alaska, we were shown the famous Alaskan oil pipeline. Alaska is a region which is susceptible to earthquakes. Therefore, those pipelines were set up in such a way as to cause them to flex and give should there be movement of the earth. Otherwise, there would have been countless breaks and oil leaks.

Our tall skyscrapers are made of powerful steel with just enough *flexibility* so that, if hurricanes, tornadoes, or even earthquakes were to strike, there would be enough pliability to keep the buildings from breaking apart. The trait that will help us to withstand the storms of life is the ability to bend and give without breaking apart. We urgently need to acquire the willingness to adapt to the various phases of life, because change is inevitable.

An old Eastern proverb says, "No man steps into the same river twice." Indeed, the river's water will rush on, and no one can stop it or stand in the exact same water again.

Planning for Change

It's nice that at least some of life's changes are those for which one can plan, such as the birth of a baby. A couple will have known for about nine months that a bundle of joy is coming, and still there will be a period of adjustment. Most new parents are not quite prepared to believe that life will never be the same again. No more sleeping late! In fact, sometimes it almost means no more sleeping at all! They cannot just go out spontaneously for the evening anymore, and that's just the beginning. Then comes the terrible twos when housekeeping starts to get tough. There are doctors' appointments and, eventually, music lessons, soccer games, carpooling, and the teenage years. Yes, this "baby event" is a permanent change, but it's one for which we can plan.

Another change for which we can actually plan is the "empty nest." For years the house will have been buzzing and shaking with teenagers and their friends, but suddenly, it falls strangely *quiet*. For some parents, this is a devastating change. Others find it quite nice. No matter how the parent reacts to this change, it is, at least, one that every parent should be able to foresee. The same is true of retirement. Many people have difficulty adjusting to that new style of life, even though they should have had many years to expect it. Even a change as devastating as the loss of a spouse is one that can be expected to some degree. With few exceptions, wives do outlive

> *"No man steps into the same river twice."*
> —EASTERN PROVERB

their husbands. So most wives vaguely suspect that they will someday experience widowhood.

Bob and I had expected that, at some point, I would be left without him. There was some difference in our ages, and he was genetically predisposed to heart disease. His younger brother, who is exactly my age, had a heart attack when he was only forty-five years old. That certainly got our attention!

Since we were aware of the possibility of early heart problems, we talked about it and put our business affairs in order. Bob took early retirement from the bank, we sold our large house, and traveled extensively during the last years of his life. In our wildest imagination, we would never have thought that his life would end the way it did. Yet, the talking and preparing had been done, and all of that preparation has helped me immeasurably during this transition time.

I have come to believe that an important part of accepting any change that can even vaguely be expected is to have talked about it and to have made some specific preparation. A certain percentage of people are so fearful of change that they will refuse to do this, especially if the expected change has to do with death. It is out of their comfort zone. Some almost feel as if talking about it might hasten the reality. Death, however, need not be such a frightening subject to a Christian. After all, it is the happiest transition of all, but *failing to plan* for it can cause some difficult transition problems for those who are left behind.

Therefore, any life change that can be expected should be *thought about, studied, and discussed.* If you have children approaching the teenage years, why not start reading materials on that subject. Learn about the hormonal changes that will be taking place—changes that may dramatically affect their dispositions. You will understand them better, and perhaps you can help them to better understand themselves.

If you have aging parents for whom you may have some responsibility, read what is available today about assisted living. There are a number of new options available, such as home health-care. It might even help to learn about disposition changes that may be expected in an aging parent. Don't just assume that it will all fall into place. It may just all fall apart! Whatever happens, you will move through it more comfortably if you expect it and prepare for it. Any change that can be expected is one for which a person can prepare.

Surprise Changes

Those are some of the changes that can be expected, but there are some changes that come like a sudden explosion, and there is *no* planning for them. It can take only a second for your life to be irreversibly changed. You may suddenly be bolted into an environment of survival, like a fish thrown onto dry ground, trying to breathe air that can't be breathed!

There was a man in the Bible whose life was moving along right on schedule. Everything was going according to plan.

> *Don't just assume that it will all fall into place. It may just all fall apart!*

There was no reason to believe that he would be anything but an important leader. This young Jewish man of Tarsus was highly educated. He had learned at the feet of the esteemed teacher, Gamaliel. Acts 26:10 causes some scholars to think that he was already a member of the prestigious Sanhedrin. Well known and highly respected, he, no doubt, had a host of friends and relatives in the Jewish community. This was Saul of Tarsus.

Saul could not have planned for his life change, because it came suddenly and without warning. During a stunning encounter on the road to Damascus, he was blinded—physically blinded! In a terrible predicament, he was actually put into the hands of those whom he had meant to arrest. His life was turned upside down. He had been made *physically blind* so that he might *see spiritually.* He actually became one of the people he had been persecuting. What a *change!* How could anyone be flexible enough to adapt to such a dramatic change? His change meant big trouble. The Jews wanted to kill him, and the Christians were afraid of him.

Do you think Saul had any personal adjustment to make in all this? He had lost friends and probably was disowned by his family. His life would never be what he had dreamed it would be. It's not easy to give up a dream. I believe that he did have an adjustment. Acts 9:30 says that the disciples sent him to Tarsus, because his life was in danger, but notice this: Saul did not reappear until Barnabas went *looking for him* (Acts 11:25). No one knows the exact length of time that Saul spent in seclusion, but it was very possibly a time of coming to grips with an *awesome change* that had happened in his life. Barnabas found him and brought him to Antioch. The rest is history.

Saul (even his name changed to Paul) moved on with his new life—not on to power and prosperity—but on to peace and productivity. There is none other like him among the apostles of Jesus.

Adjustment to a major change is more comfortable if things move in an upward mode—that is, if things are getting better. In Paul's case, he went from being respected to being despised. It was necessary for him to find a new niche for himself and make new friends. Sometimes that is exactly the kind of change with which people wrestle. Paul proved *flexible* enough to cope with all those problems, and I believe that the source of that flexibility was God himself. That same source can help us to accept change, too.

Moving On

Frequently, when there has been a major change, such as the one described in Paul's life, people will deeply yearn for the "good old days." There's something about looking back at times gone by that causes us to believe that things were better than they may have really been. Sometimes, we will emotionally shackle ourselves to the past—to that time before the change. We may cling to lost dreams to such an extent that we don't move on with life. This shows that we have not acquired the characteristic of flexibility.

An Old Testament character poignantly exemplifies how the human mind longs for a time from the past. Listen to a few passages from chapter twenty-nine of Job:

- "How I long for the months gone by, for the days when God watched over me" (Job 29:2).
- "When my path was drenched with cream" (Job 29:6).
- "When I went to the gate of the city and took my seat in the public square" (Job 29:7).
- "Young men saw me and stepped aside" (Job 29:8).

Job is reminiscing about a happier time when he was a highly respected man. Now, listen as he contrasts that glorious time with the present time, filled with pain and disdain:

- "But now they mock me, men younger than I" (Job 30:1).
- "They detest me and keep their distance" (Job 30:10).
- "Terrors overwhelm me. My dignity is driven away by the wind. My safety vanishes like a cloud" (Job 30:15).

My heart hurts for Job as I read those sad passages, but his thoughts are a perfect example of someone who is trying in vain to recapture the past.

So what is the formula for accepting irreversible change? What is the adjustment process? There is a formula laid out for us by the apostle Paul, who had once been that young man called Saul. Much later, in Philippians 3:13 he said, *"Forgetting what is behind* and straining toward what is ahead, *I press on toward the goal* to win the prize for which God has called me heavenward in Christ Jesus" (emphasis mine).

Paul's formula was to (1) let go of the past, and (2) move on with a goal, or with purpose. Instead of dwelling on the past or on some dream that will not come to pass, he urges his hearers to *press on, move on.* We must admit to ourselves that we are in a new phase of life and that, this too, is a road that must be traveled.

I heard a speaker at a seminar last year tell about her early days of widowhood. She said that some friends invited her to dinner, along with another lady, who had been a widow for eighteen years. She assumed that her friends were hoping that the other widow would be an encouragement to her. Wrong! Instead, this more experienced widow cried through soup, salad, the main course, and dessert!

The newly widowed lady said, "In a way, she *did* motivate me, because I promised myself that in eighteen years I would not still be a grieving widow."

Right then, she decided that it would be much more appropriate to put the past behind her and move forward, and she did! She became a college professor and has authored several books.

Such a variety of roadblocks can make it necessary for you to alter your course. If you were traveling down a highway and suddenly saw a road block or a detour sign, would you just stop and go home? Probably you would try to find another way to get to your destination. You may have to take an unfamiliar road. You may have some difficulty and discomfort. Or you might even get temporarily lost. You might think, *If only that detour had not been there!* But if you keep trying, you will likely reach your destination.

Paul put his roadblocks behind him, made the changes, shifted gears, and pressed on toward his goal—heaven. And that's our goal too, isn't it? I don't know about you, but I have found that keeping my eye on heaven really helps my flexibility in overcoming life's roadblocks.

> *Keeping my eye on heaven really helps my flexibility in overcoming life's roadblocks.*

As Jesus ascended into the heavens, the apostles stood there transfixed. This was their leader. What was to become of them now? Talk about change! These men had already been in transition for three years. Now their leader was gone. This was not how they had dreamed it would be. Suddenly, two men dressed in white spoke to them: "Why are you standing here looking up into the sky?" It was time to *move on.* Things would never be the same for them again. They were no longer in their comfort zone, but they must not look back. The Lord had great plans for these men.

Can we prepare ourselves emotionally and spiritually to *move on,* even though major change may come as we make this temporary journey? Yes, we can. True, it will be harder for some of us than for others, but if we start preparing ourselves, our ability to roll with the punches might just surprise us.

Growing in Flexibility

Here are a few suggestions for growing the trait of flexibility:

1. Work on your *perspective* **about what life really is.**
Life is a sojourn, not an end in itself. It is temporary at best. So
what if we have to endure some adjustments along the way?
The difficulties of this life serve as reminders that we should
not feel so comfortable with this world. Let's try not to attach
undue importance to this journey. It's only a means to a glorious
end—heaven. Paul said in 2 Timothy 4:18, "The Lord will
rescue me from every evil attack and will bring me safely to his
heavenly kingdom." However, even in this life, we can have
more joy if we keep that perspective.

2. Try to look for the signs of *hope* **when change seems
unpleasant.** View change as a new opportunity. As mentioned
earlier, God has a way of bringing good out of evil, strength
out of weakness, and success out of failure. Give some thought
to *what could be worse* than this change. You usually don't have
to look very far before discovering that things could be much
worse. First Thessalonians 5:18 says, "Give thanks in all circumstances." It is likely that in almost any circumstance of this
life, we still have *something* for which to be thankful. I know I do.

3. Be interested in other people. As you journey
through this life, don't travel alone. Especially in the Lord, it is
people that make the difference between joy and despair. In
Galatians 6:2 we are admonished to "carry each other's burdens." Involvement in the lives of other people teaches us valuable lessons about accepting change.

4. Learn new things. Keep a variety of interests. Don't
be so consumed in one area that there is no other. It may tax
your comfort zone to learn new things; however, the more you
learn, the more flexible you are able to be. New experiences
help to overcome that natural fear of the unknown.

**5. Work toward keeping God as the center of your
life.** The Lord is the only one in this life that cannot be taken
away. He is the only thing that does not change. Some people

have possessions as the center of their lives, but possessions can
vanish overnight. It is often our children that tend to be the
center of our lives, but even they can be lost. Most of the time
they grow up and have lives of their own. For some, it is their
spouse or pleasures or prestige, but all those can change or be
taken away. It is only our God that we can be absolutely sure
will always be there and never change. We must make sure that
He is the center of our lives!

   6. Keep your eye on your final destination. When all
is said and done, the only thing that will matter is whether we
got where we were trying to
go. We are attached to this
earthly life because it is the
only experience that we know
first-hand. Our human logic
binds us to this time and place.
God, however, draws us to a
heightened awareness that
physical ills, divorce, bankruptcy, and death are concerns which
should be superseded by our desire to be at home with Him.
Such an awareness lessens the fear of life's storms. That's what
Paul meant when he said, "I consider that our present sufferings
are not worth comparing with the glory that will be revealed
in us" (Romans 8:18). He also said in 2 Corinthians 4:17, "For
our light and momentary troubles are achieving for us an eternal
glory that far outweighs them all."

   If you have difficulty with change, perhaps at least some
of these suggestions might help to better prepare you for some
of the major changes that may lie ahead.

> *"Things turn out best for those who make the best of the way things turn out."*

God and Change

   God's hand is in change. In Daniel 2:21 we read "He
changes the times and seasons; he sets up kings and deposes

them." God has been running things for a long time. It is likely that He has it right.

In a writing called "Illusions," the author of *Jonathan Livingston Seagull* wrote, "There is no such thing as a problem without a gift for you in its hands." For years I have had a little saying attached to the side of my refrigerator that reads,

"Things turn out best for those
who make the best of the way
things turn out."

"In all our troubles,
my joy knows no bounds."

———

2 Corinthians 7:4

Victim of driveway robbery eulogized

By Jeffrey Weiss
Staff Writer of The Dallas Morning News

A few weeks before Easter, the friends of Robert Scott reaffirmed their belief in his resurrection.

Mr. Scott, 63, died Friday, a day after he was shot in the head while struggling with a robber in his driveway. Monday, about 1,000 people filled the Prestoncrest Church of Christ in North Dallas for a memorial service.

The congregational singing set the tone with a line from the first hymn: "I can't feel at home in this world anymore."

And pulpit minister Prentice Meador opened his "Celebration of God" by referring to the familiar passage from I Corinthians: "Death, where is your sting?"

The hourlong service only briefly touched on Mr. Scott's violent death.

"Celebration is the key to Christianity," Dr. Meador said. "We have a choice today between tragedy and joy ... between the last 60 seconds of Bob's life and the last more than 60 years of Bob's life ... between

> "Celebration is the key to Christianity. We have a choice today between tragedy and joy . . . between the last 60 seconds of Bob's life and the last more than 60 years of Bob's life . . . between revenge and forgiveness . . . between despair and hope. The haunting question people have is, where was God in all of this?"
> — Dr. Prentice Meador

revenge and forgiveness ... between despair and hope.

"The haunting question people have is, where was God in all of this?"

The answer, he said, is that God was in the same place as on another Friday about 2,000 years ago, during a crucifixion.

"On that day, the horror was just as great," Dr. Meador said. "But Friday is not all there is. Sunday comes after Friday."

God was still in control, he said.

"He's the kind of God who goes to work when death has done his worst," he said. "He's the kind of God who opens tombs."

Dr. Meador was followed by George Bailey, a close friend of Mr. Scott's.

Mr. Bailey praised the staff of Parkland Memorial Hospital, where Mr. Scott was taken after the Thursday night shooting and where he died.

Like the minister, Mr. Bailey focused on the afterlife, rather than the way Mr. Scott died.

"The man who closed the door for Bob on Earth just blasted open the door to heaven," Mr. Bailey said.

Police have made no arrests in connection with Mr. Scott's slaying. However, police say the killer may

be connected to four people arrested and charged with a series of similar robberies since January.

Mr. Bailey recounted his memories of a dear friend: church cofounder; retired banker who passed his CPA exam on the first try; a man who liked to tease more than be teased, to play golf and fish, to build furniture for his grandchildren.

The spiritual theme of Monday's service was appropriate for a man who recently took a mission trip to Romania and who was supposed to be teaching Sunday school this quarter, his friend said.

A week ago Sunday, Mr. Scott had taught a class in a church on South Padre Island, where he and his wife had a winter home.

"Bob liked to fish, but he was also a fisher of men," Mr. Bailey said.

He told the crowd that some had come from Illinois, Oklahoma and Nebraska to share their feelings for Mr. Scott at the service.

"You don't measure a man by the influence others have on him," Mr. Bailey told the crowd, "but by the influence he had on others."

CHAPTER

3

Looking for the Best Keeps Us Buoyant

IT MAY SEEM impossible to believe that even while trying to struggle through an overwhelming disaster, it is possible that some positives can always be found if we look for them. The reason I believe the trait of *looking for the positives* is one of the essentials for coping with adversity is because I found myself doing that very thing during some of the darkest days of 1994. And I did it without being conscious of it. Almost every day there was at least one thing especially encouraging that would happen.

For example, when it was felt by most that I should have some protection, a wonderful Christian police officer, who actually attended my home church, volunteered for that duty. She slept in the bedroom next to mine for several months, and we became good friends. What a wonderful blessing!

Also during that time, the children and I were sitting in our attorney's office going over some business when he mentioned that the accountant whom he was recommending would be stopping by to meet me momentarily. Soon the young CPA came in, and as soon as the attorney left the room for a moment, he leaned over and said, "Mrs. Scott, I am a Christian, and I knew Bob." Suddenly, my spirits were lifted unbelievably!

Those are only two examples of the daily blessings that God used to soothe my bruised emotions. Just the right people always seemed to be there at just the right time, as well as countless other positives, some of which were rather small things. Often they were the kinds of things that I could have failed to even notice, unless it had always been my inclination to cling to the positives.

Laughing in the Face of Trouble

Even being able to find humor or reason to laugh is so therapeutic during stressful times. I remember one evening when an undercover agent stopped in to visit with me. He had called before coming, and the police officer answered my door when he rang. Because I had known his family for many years, we had a nice visit. He had been spending some time watching my house.

> *"We are hard pressed on every side, but not crushed; perplexed, but not in despair; persecuted, but not abandoned; struck down, but not destroyed."*

As he prepared to leave, we all became aware that a lot of activity was going on in front of my house. All of us were a bit alarmed at first. It seems that in his undercover role, he had been driving an old car with Louisiana license plates, and its windows were darkened. The regular police patrol had spotted that suspicious-looking car parked near my house, and they had surrounded it. They had their flashlights out and were trying to see inside the car. One of the officers was on the radio calling in the license number. The young undercover agent went scrambling out to reclaim his vehicle. Our laughter at the irony of the situation really made me feel much more like my usual self.

Even in the midst of tragedy, finding a reason to laugh can bring a little healing. It would be wise to start noticing and focusing on some of the small blessings that come your way every day and be thankful for them.

Focus on the Up Side

The apostle Paul gave us all some very good lessons in learning to look for the best. It is he who said, "In all our troubles, my joy knows no bounds" (2 Corinthians 7:4). Please notice his blazing spirit and his propensity to focus on the positive side of a dark situation. In 2 Corinthians 4:8–9, he said: "We are hard pressed on every side, but not crushed; perplexed, but not in despair; persecuted, but not abandoned; struck down, but not destroyed."

Paul was not blind to the fact that he was having a problem, but he chose to see that there were some positives, in spite of his difficulties. Therefore, it is Paul who is qualified to tell us that we should train ourselves to focus on the *up* side of things. In Philippians 4:8, he is teaching us that we should be preparing our minds to look for the best when he says: "Finally, brothers, whatever is true, whatever is noble, whatever is right, whatever is pure, whatever is lovely, whatever is admirable—if anything is excellent or praiseworthy—*think about such things.*"

Is that what you practice? Or do you focus on flaws? Do you focus on faults or admirable qualities in others? Do you focus on what is going right or what is going wrong?

Paul must have been aware that he modeled an optimistic attitude before these Philippians because he told them to put into practice what they had seen in him. That is bold! Then he tells them what their reward will be if they develop the trait of looking for the best. He said, "And the God of peace will be with you."

Peace is what we all want, but are we willing to go into serious training to get it? If someone were selling peace of mind, we would definitely be buying. Paul is promising it as a reward for those who have trained themselves to look for the best in their circumstances of life. (You begin to see why self-control is also on the list of traits necessary when preparing for adversity).

Permanent or Temporary?

People who allow themselves to think negative thoughts will likely become pessimistic. Pessimists view every little setback as *permanent*. Those people often blame themselves or maybe someone else or even God! People who develop such an outlook tend to view any unpleasant circumstance as hopeless and avoid focusing on any good thing that may come their way.

People who are able to look for positives, even when there are serious problems, are optimists. They view setbacks as *temporary* and as something that can and will be worked through. Then they commit to working through it.

Dr. John Schindler once said, "Happiness is a state of mind in which our thinking is pleasant a good share of the time." Often people go all through life waiting to find just the *right stage* of life. They are waiting for some nebulous time when they will finally be happy. It is then that they believe they will be positive, optimistic, and cheerful. Young women think it will be when they get married. Married women think it will be when they have children. Then they think it will be when the children have grown up. Then, they think it will be when they retire. By that time, they have trained themselves to search for, but never quite find, true happiness.

Being happy and optimistic usually go together, and it's much better if we can develop that attitude early in life. A friend of mine once told me that her mother made her read *Pollyanna* about four or five times while she was growing up. No doubt, that mother was trying to instill in her daughter a spirit of optimism, and it worked.

If I were to ask each of you to tell what adversity you have suffered, we would hear some heart-wrenching stories. Who is to say which crisis is worse? Actually it doesn't matter which trouble is worse. What really makes the difference is what we do with the problem.

> *Happiness is not something that happens to you. It's something that you do.*

If you want to have a joyful, peaceful, and productive life, you must reach the conclusion that it is not *what* roadblocks are in the path. The question is, "Am I going to stay the course?" Happiness is not something that *happens* to you. It's something that you *do*. Only *you* can control the way you think. Good is real, and evil is real. Upon which one do you want to focus your mind?

The Happiness Habit

The way that we view things that go on around us can become a habit. Dr. Maxwell Maltz once said, "Our habits are garments worn by our personalities." Our responses and reactions to problems are habits that we have learned to perform, automatically, without having to think or decide. It is thought that about 95 percent of our behavior and response is habit. For instance, we back the car out of the garage and close the garage door. This has become such a habit that we get two blocks away and wonder whether we closed the garage door.

I mentioned previously that parents sometimes affect our response to adversity. In our younger years we learned that certain responses and attitudes were appropriate. Some of our responses turn out to be not so desirable after all. Sometimes we have developed the habit of fault-finding or focusing on negatives, and those habits do not serve us well.

The good news is that habits can be changed. It *does* require a conscious decision and a lot of practice, but it can be done! I don't believe the scriptures ever tell us to do something that cannot be done. They always tell us to do things that are good for us. Therefore, when Paul told us in Philippians 4 to think about lovely things, admirable things, and good reports, he was obviously telling us to do something that we have the ability to do and something that the Lord knows will serve us well in this life.

> *"Men are disturbed, not by the things that happen, but by their opinions of the things that happen."*

Preparing yourself to think in the way that Paul was proposing is well worth the effort for a wide variety of reasons. A Russian psychologist tested people when they were thinking pleasant thoughts and unpleasant thoughts. He found that when they were thinking pleasant thoughts:

- They could see better.
- They could smell better.
- They could hear better.
- They could detect finer differences in touch.

Dr. Margaret Corbett has found that memory improves. Dr. William Bates' test showed that the improvement in eyesight was immediate. Tests have also shown that all internal organs function better when we are thinking happy thoughts. Disease reflects "dis-*ease*" in the way that we view life.

The Proverbs are filled with passages which substantiate these findings:

- "A cheerful look brings joy to the heart,
  And good news gives health to the bones." Proverbs 15:30
- "A cheerful heart is good medicine,
  But a crushed spirit dries up the bones." Proverbs 17:22

Later in the New Testament, Paul picked up the refrain by saying, "Rejoice in the Lord always. I will say it again: rejoice" (Philippians 4:4). Obviously, the Lord wanted His people to recognize the rewards of being cheerful, upbeat, positive people. A joyful and positive spirit is the music that makes us less aware of the stress of life's journey.

Thought Control

Therefore, I say again, we may not have much control over what things happen to us in this life, but we *can choose* to seize control of what our ultimate response will be. By taking control of the way we think, we can spare ourselves at least some of the pain during a time of tragedy or crisis. A wise philosopher once said, "Men are disturbed, not by the things that happen, but by *their opinions* of the things that happen." A man once lost his business and said, "I am ruined and disgraced." True, he had lost his business, but the "ruined and disgraced" were his own personal interpretations of what had happened.

After Bob's death, I was reluctant to go to his favorite restaurant. It was because of my distorted opinion of what *he* might be feeling or thinking, as if he might be somewhere wishing that he could be there with me. You see, I was adding unnecessary pain for myself by interjecting my own interpretation of the facts. In more rational moments, I knew he would much rather be where he is than to be eating at this restaurant.

In the grieving process, we are prone to add our own thoughts and emotions, even ascribing those emotions to the one who is gone. In truth, I was the one doing the missing. The missing is done by the one still making the sojourn through this life. I believe that parents who lose young children sometimes add even more pain to their grief by imagining their precious child out there somewhere all alone and feeling very homesick for the nurturing care of home and parents. Controlling the thinking process can help minimize pain during times of loss, whether it is business failure or loss of a loved one.

A positive and aggressive response in times of trouble can be very successful and rewarding. To get a plan of action and move forward with it is like good medicine. There is only one area over which you have control when the storms of life blow violently. You alone can control your response.

A mother whose child was born with Down's Syndrome in recent years decided on a plan of action. She could have responded in a number of less desirable ways, but she chose to begin her own study of her child's problem. She learned so much that she actually put together a vitamin regimen which improved her child's condition so noticeably that doctors are now studying her new procedure.

It is possible for any one of us to apply that lady's positive, aggressive approach to many of the regular problems that confront us. She refused to be defeated. That's a style of thinking which some people acquire more easily than others, but any healthy person can improve his ability to think and react in this way. We should not try to run away or hide our heads in the sand.

Don't Fret

You don't have to allow circumstances to dictate or control you. Yet, if you make a practice of being easily upset by people or incidents—even small ones—you will probably find yourself doing it consistently. In this mode, you will be unhappy a lot of the time.

As Psalm 37:1 says, "Do not fret because of evil men or be envious of those who do wrong. For like grass, they will soon wither." And in verse 8, "Refrain from anger and turn from wrath. Do not fret; it leads to evil."

When the newspapers ran the story that the defendant in our murder trial had hired a new attorney and was appealing his conviction, that was not good news for our family. I called my daughter, Michelle, and her reply put my thinking on the right path. She said, "That man has taken all from me that he's going to get. I am not going to spend the next two or three years thinking about him." How true! So we don't think about him. It was a conscious decision to go on with our lives until we know the outcome of his appeal, and we don't lie awake thinking about it. We have chosen not to fret. To prepare our minds for adversity, we can practice looking for the best, even in troublesome circumstances of life.

A young second grader charged through the front door of his home, having just completed a very bad day at school. He was not chosen to be on the team at recess, he had lost his lunch money, and Mrs. Snodgrass had given him a "C" on his homework.

As he came in, his mother said, "Jeremy, come and have some refreshments and tell me what was the best thing that happened to you today!"

The change of focus almost gave Jeremy whiplash! If someone had offered him twenty dollars, he could not have thought of a single thing that had happened to him that day that qualified as "good."

Most of us can identify with Jeremy's feelings. Occasionally, our circumstances can be so bleak that it's difficult to realize that there's still good to be recognized. However, Jeremy's mother was right on track in causing him to look for positives in his day. It would be a very good practice for all mothers to begin early in training their children to practice *looking for the best*. To say, "What did you like best about your day or your trip?" is a subtle way to train young people to look for the good things and focus more on them than the bad things.

> *The next time your day begins badly, try refocusing. Punch the reset button on your mental outlook and try to turn your day around.*

Whatever You Focus on Expands

It is important to practice focusing on the good, the lovely, and the admirable things, because *what you focus on expands*. That's why complainers never run out of things about which to complain. Just notice sometime. When you get up in the morning and spill your coffee, your hose has a run, and the car keys are nowhere to be found, the mind begins to focus on all the things that are going wrong. You decide that this is not going to be a good day, and sure enough *it's not*, because what you focus on expands. So, mishaps keep happening. The next time your day begins badly, try *refocusing*. Punch the reset button on your mental outlook and try to turn your day around.

Obviously, one of our greatest struggles to stay positive comes in the area of *relationships*. Relationships bring our greatest joys, but they also bring our greatest sorrows. It's likely that many of our heartaches could be avoided if we could train our minds to make allowances for the faults of people in our lives. Matthew 7:1–2 says, "Do not judge, or you too will be judged. For in the same way you judge others, you will be judged, and with the measure you use, it will be measured to you."

Even the best of us have some undesirable qualities that need to be overlooked, if at all possible. That being the case, we can well afford to overlook the flaws and blemishes of those with whom we associate. We *can* and *must* develop an attitude that gives others the benefit of the doubt. Most of us have a great talent for finding the faults in other people. One would almost think that God had commanded it, when He really commanded just the opposite.

One of mankind's greatest weaknesses is allowing Satan free rein over the way we think about other people. Perhaps you sometimes have negative thoughts about your spouse, such as, "He is not sensitive enough to my needs." You can practice Paul's style of thinking in such instances. Paul might say, "Not sensitive, *but* a good provider" or "Not a great provider, *but* so good with the children." The whole picture should not look negative. If it does, it possibly means that you should start working on self.

In case you doubt that we human beings tend to give Satan free rein in the way we think about people, just look at a few examples of the way we view certain Bible characters.

What about King David? When you think of him, do you remember his great kindness to Mephibosheth? Do you remember him because he so respected God's anointed, King Saul, that he would not lay a hand on him? I don't think so!

When David is mentioned, he is usually remembered for his greatest indiscretion with Bathsheba.

Do we remember Peter for having given up a lucrative fishing business to follow Jesus? Not likely! He is usually remembered for denying Christ three times or sinking when walking on water.

There is no lack of wonderful things that can be credited to both these men. It's just that most people haven't *prepared their minds* to look for the best in other people.

Even the apostle Paul, who was usually so good at looking at the positive side of things, was *ticked off* at John Mark, because he dared abandon the mission trip before it was finished. When the time came for another trip, Paul could focus only on John Mark's previous failure. So, he would not allow John Mark to go with him again. In Paul's mind, John Mark was a quitter.

It was Barnabas who chose *not to focus* on John Mark's failure. Barnabas believed that one mistake need not label John Mark for life. It was no accident that Barnabas was called the Son of Encouragement. One who will train his mind to overlook the bad traits and focus on the good ones can likely bring out the best in the people whose lives he touches.

The Mind-set Model

Jesus modeled the kind of mind-set that He wants us to have. He could focus on what was good in those who crossed His path. For example, when Jesus first saw Nathanael in John 1:43ff, He overlooked the sarcasm which Nathanael had expressed when Philip approached him about the Savior. Although Nathanael had never even met Jesus, he was ready to focus on the bad news.

Nathanael said, "Nazareth? Can anything *good* come from there?"

But Jesus, who had already seen Nathanael under the fig tree and probably knew what Nathanael had said about Him, remarked, "Here is an Israelite in whom there is nothing false" (John 1:47). Jesus looked for and found a good trait in Nathanael. How do you suppose that made Nathanael feel about himself?

If you hope to encourage some positive changes in another person, that person needs to hear some positive feedback. As one sportscaster put it, "The reason so many athletes say, 'Hi, Mom,' when being interviewed on television is because their moms are the ones who always believed in them."

You don't have to be someone's mom to look for and compliment the positive traits of a person. It's something you can do for anyone within your sphere of influence. It can be the son or daughter of one of your acquaintances. It can be a friend, a co-worker, or a relative. There are so many people out there who need someone to focus on their good attributes— someone who believes in them.

There is no shortage of critics. It doesn't require any special intelligence to be one. In fact, it is someone special who can play down the obvious negative traits and give attention to the admirable characteristics in another person. By building up others, you may be just the spark that ignites a John Mark to become a great servant of the Lord. There is no warmer feeling than to have encouraged other people toward reaching their potential.

Don't Even Think about It!

Magnifying the faults of others rarely makes problems better. Honestly, I have never known anyone's faults to be cured by a friend discussing those faults with other friends over coffee. It is possible for people to be consumed with negative thoughts about other people to the point of experiencing unhappiness and depression. The better plan would be to pray for that imperfect person. You feel much better toward any person for whom you pray. Pray for yourself, too, that you will not dwell on the undesirable traits of some person who is bothering you. Then, do your part and don't think about it.

I was driving through a neighborhood recently. So many cars were at the curb that there was no place to park. Finally,

> *"Refrain from anger and turn from wrath; do not fret— it leads only to evil."*

I saw what appeared to be a spot, but when I got there, a sign was neatly planted at the curb: "Don't Even Think About It!" That would be a very good sign to plant in our minds to chase away negative thoughts.

It might also help us to remember that people gravitate toward those who make them feel good about themselves. Perhaps the best incentive for preparing our minds to look for the best in others is this: You usually get back what you give out! Most of us know the merits of learning to look for the things that are lovely and admirable and worthy of praise.

Tools for the Task

We are not always so sure that we know how to achieve the goal. Here are a few tools for the task:

1. Read good books and other materials that help you think about the things mentioned in Philippians 4.

2. Associate with positive, upbeat people. I once had an acquaintance who called me regularly to tell me all the bad things that she thought were going on in the church. I felt as if I were drowning. It does us harm to associate with people who think that way. While it is our duty to hear people who wish to talk about their own personal problems, it is *not* our duty to hear them tear down others. We would be wise to choose for our closest friends—our Peter, James, and John friends—those who also want to learn to look for the best.

3. Have a plan of action to overcome your setbacks or adversity. Don't just hide your face. Address these issues:

    a. What do I want?
    b. What are the obstacles?
    c. Identify people who can help you.
    d. Get a specific plan of action.
    e. Punch the "Go" button!

4. Practice optimism daily. Use these techniques to help you be more optimistic:

- Determine to find something good about someone who is troublesome to you.
- Resolve to have pleasant thoughts at least the majority of the time.
- Find yourself a happy tune to hum or sing (or perhaps a good compact disk or cassette to play). However, I think there is something magical about doing your own humming or singing, even if it's not beautiful.
- Smile at least three times a day, although that's not often enough.
- Pray to the Lord to help you, because He wants you to think good thoughts. He has told you to do so! He will help you to win in this effort. Believe it!

Read Philippians 4 and Psalm 37 often. And keep hidden in your heart the words of Psalm 37:8:

"Refrain from anger and turn from wrath;
do not fret—it leads only to evil."

"Tho' he slay me,
yet will I trust him."

——

JOB 13:15, KJV

Morning News

xas, Saturday, March 26, 1994 • 6 Sections HF • • • 25 Cents

Police to charge suspect in first driveway slaying

No arrests yet in 2nd killing

By Dan R. Barber
and Nora Lopez
Staff Writers of The Dallas Morning News

A 20-year-old Dallas man was arrested Friday and held on suspicion of capital murder in the March 3 driveway robbery and slaying of a Far North Dallas man.

Patrol officers arrested Derek Andrie Haggerty about 12:30 p.m. between Maple Avenue and Harry Hines Boulevard, police spokesman Ed Spencer said Friday.

Mr. Haggerty, of the 1100 block of East Pentagon Parkway in east Oak Cliff, had not been arraigned late Friday, but police said he would be charged in the fatal shooting of Bob Scott, a retired bank executive.

"Haggerty has been a suspect in this crime for some time," Mr. Spencer said, "but only today was enough evidence developed to file a case — and

we're not saying what that is."

The suspect made the trip to the Lew Sterrett Justice Center in leg restraints after he tried to escape through a suspended ceiling at downtown police headquarters, Mr. Spencer said.

Mr. Scott, 63, was gunned down outside the garage of his home in the 5700 block of En'Core Drive as he and his wife returned from a shopping trip.

Mr. Spencer declined to say whether any other arrests were imminent in **Please see DRIVEWAY on Page 15A.**

4

Trust Overcomes Panic in the Storm

THERE WAS *one* thing that really made the difference between survival and defeat during the tragedy that changed my world. It was the ability to actually rely upon and trust in God to conduct me through the storm. It is unfortunate that we cannot be absolutely certain that this level of trust will actually function for us until it has been put to the acid test.

As a person disposed to be rather self-sufficient, I would not normally have felt like a helpless child. Yet, with the suddenness of a bolt of lightning, I had been plunged into the churning waters of a riveting robbery and murder case. Television and radio reporters, police investigators, and detectives swarmed around me. In such an atmosphere, quiet time is a rare commodity; so, when I was finally alone in the stillness of the night, I began to feel an uncharacteristic helplessness.

In that darkness, when I could lie quietly between the smooth sweet-scented sheets of my own bed, I could think about the unthinkable. I would longingly slide my hand to that empty side of the bed and think how fragile human existence really is. I would try to grasp how death could be so final. It was at that point that I was quite ready to relinquish control to someone else.

In the depths of that silent room, it became clearer to me than ever before that I had one who was more powerful than any horror that could befall me in this life. That was it! God really would be in charge of resolving all that was facing me at that time. As if His gentle hand were stroking my brow, I began to feel reassured and confident. God would get me through this storm, not with a magical stroke of a wand, but one day at a time. With complete certainty, I had found my shelter, and I slept soundly and peacefully every night.

Bob had always been such a major presence in our family. I had always relied upon his expertise and self-confidence in handling any serious problem. Our children and other family members had also turned to him for answers. I realized we would be making a number of important decisions without the advantage of his counsel. That's when my prayers flowed freely to the one who was my hope and my refuge: "Lord, I don't know if I can do this. Please lead me safely through all this turmoil that surrounds me and will not go away." Those prayers calmed and strengthened me. Each day I seemed to be given just what was needed.

Learning to Free Fall

I must emphasize that praying to God and believing that He hears my prayers was not something that I discovered only in the midst of this storm. God had been a part of my life since I was a child. While I believe that He would have been there for me even if I had only then discovered Him, I doubt that my own trust in Him would have brought me such a degree of peace and serenity if I had just met Him for the first time. We have more confidence in God's ability to see us through the storm if we have known Him for a long time. There is less panic when we have already learned to depend upon Him day by day.

When I was a child, there was a game of nerves that we sometimes played. While one friend stood behind me, I would do a free fall backward, trying to feel confident that my friend would catch me before I crashed to the floor. To perform such a backward free fall required some fortitude and no small degree of trust in the person doing the catching. I could never feel quite safe until I felt that pair of hands take hold.

Living the life of a believer has some similarity to that free fall. We have faith in God and choose to believe that God will catch us when we fall. Yet, for some of us, years of smooth sailing may go by before there is much need for rescue from a really destructive storm. In a sense, such smooth sailing may tend to weaken us.

Through the years of my life, I had occasionally experienced unpleasant situations, but mostly, my life had been very blessed. It's too bad that tragedy's deadly blow must strike before we can feel the strong hands of the Lord, catching us and gently lifting us to our feet. However, it is in the depths of disaster—when self-help is out of the question—that our trust can reap its sweetest rewards. It is a glorious and faith-building experience to helplessly depend on God and to see His power at work. I thought of His words to Paul in 2 Corinthians 12:9: "My power is made perfect in weakness."

Waterfall Trust

The ability to *genuinely* trust in God can be our most stabilizing force when there is a storm in this life. However, genuine trust is not a trait that we just automatically acquire. It requires much more than merely giving mental assent to the existence of God. It is much more than faithful church attendance. In order to be able to genuinely trust in God to catch us when there is serious trouble, we need to have been practicing an ongoing relationship with Him through years of prayer and attention to His Word.

To say that we "trust in the Lord" is a phrase that rolls easily off the tongue, *but do we really?* We hear people say it all the time, but do we really understand that phrase?

> *Trust means that we believe God does not make mistakes.*

There once was an acrobat who had mastered the art of walking the high wire. A wire was stretched high above a gigantic waterfall, and a large crowd gathered to watch him perform this feat.

As he climbed the ladder to the top, he called to the crowd below: "How many of you believe that I can walk this wire across the waterfall?"

The crowd below roared its confidence that he could.

Then he lifted a wheel barrow and asked, "How many of you believe that I can walk this wheel barrow across the wire over the falls?"

The crowd below shouted, "Yes, yes, we think you can!"

Then he asked, "Who will volunteer to ride in the wheel barrow?"

Silence. It's easy to say to the Lord, "I think you can," but when our world comes crashing in around us, what will we say then?

The more we doubt God and His ability or His willingness to rescue us and see us through the storms of life, the more fear, worry, and insecurity we will experience. Trust means that we believe God does not make mistakes. Romans 8:6 says, "The mind controlled by the spirit is life and peace." I believe that peace is directly proportionate to our ability to genuinely trust God.

Stay on Board

When we are enveloped in a really violent storm, we often feel a desperate need to escape. Like being locked up in a house of horrors, we sense an urgency to break free into the fresh air and sunlight. In Acts 27, when Paul was aboard a ship that was being battered by a violent storm, he had to try to calm the sailors on that ship. Those men felt panic and wanted to jump overboard.

Paul said to the centurion and the soldiers, "Unless these men stay with the ship, you cannot be saved." Those men trusted Paul's advice. Trust always involves an element of risk, but when calamity batters our ship, it is essential that we have enough trust to stay on board and ride out the

> *When calamity batters our ship, it is essential that we have enough trust to stay on board and ride out the storm.*

storm. Jesus said in John 14:21, "Do not let your hearts be troubled. Trust in God; trust also in me."

People who find comfort in God's Word almost always turn to the psalms of David when they are facing adversity. What is there about the writings of David that draw the suffering ones? I believe it is David's utter trust in God to see him through his trials. David seemed to be completely confident that God would supply what he needed. Do you think that David suddenly developed that kind of trust the moment he saw Goliath? Of course not. David had been learning to rely on God when he was just an inconspicuous shepherd boy. Listen to 1 Samuel 17:34ff as David speaks to King Saul in the Valley of Elah:

> Your servant has been keeping his father's sheep. When a lion or a bear came and carried off a sheep from the flock, I went

after it, struck it, and rescued it from its mouth. . . . Your servant has killed both the lion and the bear; this uncircumcised Philistine will be like one of them, because he has defied the armies of the living God. The Lord who delivered me from the paw of the lion and the paw of the bear will deliver me from the hand of this Philistine.

David had always given credit to the Lord for his victories. He didn't spontaneously decide to rely on God in the face of the greatest storm of his life. David was mentally prepared to trust God *before* adversity arose. And then he stayed on board, no matter what storm arose.

> *Some people think they can know God by just living, breathing, and giving mental assent to His existence. It doesn't work that way! God reveals himself through His Word—the Holy Scripture.*

If we, then, have learned to rely on God in the daily skirmishes, in the small private crises, then when the major storm strikes us, it will be much easier to believe that God will see us through it as well. We cannot wait until the storm hits to make our preparation. We must begin trusting God one day at a time with little things. Faith and trust cannot be administered like aspirin, only when there is pain—although it's quite commonly tried by people in the midst of personal disasters. If trust has not been with a person on a daily basis, he will not likely be able to rely on that resource as part of his survival kit when crisis comes, and it *will* come.

God of the Book

In addition to relying on God with our everyday skirmishes and crediting Him with our daily victories, we grow strong trust in God by really getting to know Him through His Word. Some people think they can know God by just living, breathing, and giving mental assent to His existence. It doesn't work that way! God reveals himself through His Word—the Holy Scripture.

However, some people who seem to know scripture still don't know God. May I suggest that you not only read scripture often, but as you read it, listen carefully to it for your own personal messages. Concentrate on what God is telling you about himself. You cannot grow the kind of trust about which we are speaking without getting to know the personality of God, because you cannot *trust* someone you don't know.

As an example, what if you are driving down a road and hear the sickening sound of a flat tire? As you pull the car onto the shoulder of the road, another car pulls in behind you, and a man unknown to you walks toward your car. What will you do?

1. You check to be sure your door is locked.
2. You roll down your window only about an inch.
3. Then you likely decline his offer of help.

The fact is, we don't trust someone we don't know.

So, how did David get to know God so well that he believed God was really working in his life in very visible ways? He learned to trust God in the same way that you can learn to trust Him—by studying His Word. Listen to David as he speaks in Psalm 119:97: "O how love I your law. I meditate on it all day long."

The results of David's devotion to the Word of God are obvious as we read further in Psalm 119. The 114th verse says, "You are my refuge and my shield. I have put my hope in your word." Through the Word, David discovered that God's providential care was with him day and night. He realized that God was one upon whom he could depend. His God was not one who lived far above all the planets. His God was right there on the battlefield when the enemy attacked. And David could confidently say, "You are my refuge and my shield." Indeed, David learned to trust God because he *knew* Him intimately through His Word.

In the New Testament, Paul wrote to the Christians at Rome in Romans 10:2–3, explaining why the Israelites did not have faith and why the Gentiles had been able to attain righteousness: "For I can testify about them [the Israelites] that they are zealous for God, but their zeal is not based on *knowledge*. Since they did not know the righteousness that comes from God and *sought to establish their own,* they did not submit to God's righteousness."

So, we see that David had something that his people, the Israelites, did not have. He had real knowledge of God through the Word of God. Since the Israelites did not have knowledge of God, they made up their *own way* to live. Of course, their own way did not produce faith and trust in God. Instead, they trusted, not God, but their own works.

Our American culture is similar to the Israelites in that it is known for doing its *own thing.* We Americans like to feel that we have the right to think for ourselves, without the constraints of holy scripture to "cramp our style." We are so self-sufficient that we think, "I can do all things—not with God's help—but *by myself.*" In fact, the lady in the flat-tire scenario I described earlier might just be able to change that tire all by herself! It would be interesting to watch that same scene with a little twist.

What if the lady in the car declines the offer for help made by the strange man. Then a nice-looking mature *couple* stops, and the gentleman offers to help. She feels much more comfortable with this nice-looking elderly man and woman. So, she accepts their offer to help. He changes the tire, and she goes on her way. I wonder how many of us in that situation would reflect on God's providence in sending that nice, safe couple to us right when we needed to be rescued?

An incident like that one is a *lesser* crisis we could use to practice trusting that God is our refuge as David did. Our trust in God will grow if we will be more *aware* that God is working in our lives every day through His providential care.

David's trusting faith was meant to be an example for us. We can grow that kind of trust in the same way that David did—in a daily way:

- First, by really getting to know God through His Word by carefully studying, meditating, and listening for personal messages.
- Second, by *crediting God* with our victories. We probably would be wise to keep a private record of things we believe God has done for us. It has often been suggested that we keep a record of our prayer requests, because doing so is such a faith-builder. Perhaps, if we kept a journal of "every good and perfect gift" that comes from God, we would learn to trust Him and rely on Him more. Just purchase a small notebook and make an assessment at the end of each day.

I urge you to nurture your trust in God *before* you are faced with serious calamity. Trust is a major goal as we prepare for adversity.

Trust Him Anyway

In Daniel 3, on the day that King Nebuchadnezzar made an image to be worshipped, Shadrach, Meshach, and Abednego were in crisis. They were assured that, if they didn't obey his command to worship the image, the king would have them thrown into a fiery furnace.

The young men in this story bravely replied to the king, "If we are thrown into the blazing furnace, the God we serve is *able* to save us from it, and he *will* rescue us from your hand, O King. But *even if he does not . . . .*" In essence what they are saying is, "Even if our God does not save us, *we will serve Him anyway.*" I wonder how many of us can say that when bad things start happening to us.

> *Life has its fiery furnaces. At some point you will find yourself in one, whether or not you have learned to trust God to be with you. But I guarantee that the furnace will feel a lot hotter without Him.*

The three young men were bound and thrown into the furnace, which was made so hot that it actually killed the guards who threw them in.

In a little while the king took a look and said, "Weren't there just three of those men?"

"Yes," replied the servants.

"Well, I see four now, and the fourth one looks like a son of the gods."

They were actually walking around in the fire!

Nebuchadnezzar went to the opening and shouted, "Shadrach, Meshach, Abednego! Servants of the most high God! Come Out!"

So they walked out before all the advisors and officials. And guess what? They may have felt the heat, but not a hair of their heads was singed. Nor were their bodies harmed. Although God had not kept them out of that furnace, He had been right in there with them!

Life has its fiery furnaces. At some point in this life *you* will likely find yourself in one, whether or not you have learned to trust God to be with you. But I guarantee that furnace will feel a lot hotter without Him.

It's thrilling to see how God was glorified by the trust of Shadrach, Meshach, and Abednego. In Daniel 3:28, listen to that godless king speak:

> Then Nebuchadnezzar said, "Praise be to the God of Shadrach, Meshach and Abednego, who sent his angel and rescued his servants! They *trusted in him* and defied the king's command and were willing to give up their lives rather than serve or worship any god except their own God."

God is glorified when His people trust Him and when *other people see that trust.*

Although in this story of the fiery furnace, the trust exhibited by these three young men was immediately rewarded, the scriptures are filled with examples of people whose trust was just as great, and yet, they endured great punishment and pain. Shadrach, Meshach, and Abednego had indicated that if God didn't rescue them, they would *trust Him anyway.*

There were others whose trust was also put to the test. For example, Paul, whose thorn was *not* removed and who suffered prison, beatings, and shipwreck, *trusted God anyway.*

And there was Job, who had prayed for his children, but they died. It was not God who caused their deaths; it was Satan. As far as we know, Job never knew what had brought about his suffering. He just held onto his faith and said, "Tho' he slay me, yet will I trust him" (Job 13:15, KJV). We see that God rewarded that trust by blessing him with even more than he had before his adversity.

There is a long list of Bible heroes, including John the Baptist, Stephen, and Jesus Christ, who did feel the heat of adversity and died maintaining their trust in God. John the Baptist prepared the way for Jesus. He faithfully preached a very unpopular doctrine. He took no credit for himself but gave all the glory to the Christ. In Matthew 14:1–12 we read that he was put into prison and eventually beheaded. He definitely felt the pain of adversity without losing his trust. So far as we know, he never asked why.

Acts 6 and 7 tell the dramatic story of Stephen, the first Christian martyr. Those two chapters describe Stephen's character. It is obvious that he was faithful and zealous to do the work of the Lord. He was one of the seven special men chosen to serve the church. He preached a beautiful, panoramic sermon to the Jews to show them how God had worked through them as a people. In spite of all the good that Stephen had done, God allowed him to be stoned to death. No doubt, Stephen felt great pain, but he *trusted God anyway.* He didn't even ask, "Is this fair?"

Most notable among those who trusted God in the face of adversity is Jesus Christ—the gentle, kind, and sinless one. Even though He was God's own Son, He was allowed to feel the pain of adversity. He was beaten, spit upon, ridiculed, and finally crucified. We know that He felt that pain in our place. Was it fair? Sometimes fairness may not be in our best interest.

I like this poem by Herbert A. White.

A Living Faith

I've dreamed many dreams that never came true,
I've seen them vanish at dawn.

But I've realized enough of my dreams, thank God,
To make me want to dream on.

I've prayed many prayers when no answer came
Though I waited patient and long,
But answers have come to enough of my prayers
To make me keep praying on.

I've trusted many a friend that failed,
And left me to weep alone,
But I've found enough of my friends true blue,
To make me keep trusting on.

I've sown many seeds that fell by the way
For the birds to feed upon,
But I've held enough golden sheaves in my hands
To make me keep sowing on.

I've drained the cup of disappointment and pain
And gone many days without song,
But I've sipped enough nectar from the roses of life
To make me want to live on.

As we become better acquainted with God through His Word, we can more readily accept the fact that He is definitely in control, even when we don't understand our tragedies. Having read God's response to Job's questions, I felt no need to repeat the same questions. Somehow, the compulsion to ask why in the face of my calamity was not so strong. Psalm 34:15 tells us this: "For the eyes of the Lord are on the righteous, and his ears are attentive to their prayers." God is very aware of our difficulties and is able to get us through the storm, if we have the trust to allow Him to be at the helm of our ship.

When we walk with Him daily giving Him credit for being the giver of "every good and perfect gift" (James 1:17), and we credit Satan with the troubles and sufferings, then our minds

will be better prepared for any storm that blows our way. We'll
have battened down the hatches.

Rescued by Relationships

I remember when my grandfather died. I was eight years
old, and he died at our home; so, I was fairly close to all the
activity surrounding his
death—a completely normal
death. Yet, it was my first experience with losing a close
relative. I remember my child-
ish fear and insecurity. I kept
thinking how dreadful it
would be if *my* daddy were to
die. I remember distinctly
thinking that the only thing
that could help me survive
such a disaster would be some other very special and happy
relationship with someone else.

> *Cling to your trust
> in God like you
> would a life
> preserver, because
> someday it just
> may be!*

It still amazes me that such a solution would cross my
mind at eight years old, because that is exactly the answer. The
thing that is required to survive the worst blows life has to
offer is, indeed, a very special and happy relationship. And the
relationship that enables us to cope is the one that we have with
our Lord.

The prophet Jeremiah put it this way:

> *Blessed is the man who trusts in the Lord,*
>   *whose confidence is in him.*
> *He will be like a tree planted by the water*
>   *that sends out its roots by the stream.*
> *It does not fear when heat comes;*
>   *its leaves are always green.*

It has no worries in a year of drought
and never fails to bear fruit.
Jeremiah 17:7–8

Cling to your trust in God like you would a life preserver, because someday it just may be!

"*Praise be to the God and Father
of our Lord Jesus Christ,
the Father of compassion
and the God of all comfort,
who comforts us in all our troubles,
so that we can comfort those
in any trouble with the comfort
we ourselves have received from God.*"

—

2 CORINTHIANS 1:4

Bob Scott's death: It's time to take a stand, his neighbor says

Editor's note: The following guest column was written by Bill Pepper, a Northside resident and the former next door neighbor to Bob Scott, the 63-year-old man whose tragic death is reported in the above stories.

Pepper is a former executive editor of the *Gainesville* (Fla.) *Daily Sun* and was president of the Managing Editors of the State of Florida in 1960-61.

By Bill Pepper

The tragic loss of Bob Scott at the hands of an indiscriminate armed robber in his driveway March 3 is an event that should not soon be forgotten by citizens in Dallas and Fort Worth. Mr. Scott was a personal friend, a former next door neighbor and a dedicated Christian who had worked hard all of his life and given generously of his time and means to aid children of the hopeless in this area and overseas. At a memorial service Monday, March 7, packed with influential friends and recipients of his open-handed help alike, the service was given over to what minister Prentice Meador termed a "celebration of life." Sixty-two years of life in which Bob Scott had benefitted hundreds was the occasion as Dr. Meador pointed out, and not the wretched 60-plus seconds it took for a robber to waste this priceless life.

Bob Scott would be the first to forgive – that was his nature. But this community can hardly overlook its responsibility in moving to prevent future such tragedies.

As earlier stated, the above would be only the start of a suggested list of get tough measures designed to return our community to a place of reasonable peace and safety. Bob Scott, as a devoted Christian, might well have forgiven his killer, but society at large must take admittedly stringent measures to check the rampant violence which thoughtlessly denies the community another 14 or 20 years of service from this good man and others like him.

5

Caring for the Wounded

ABOUT SIX MONTHS after our tragedy, I was invited to lead a grief *recovery* group, which I consider to be more than a *support* group. We studied some material that gave us insight into the grieving process. Our group met together once a week for about two months, and we learned some very important information that would benefit almost anyone who has experienced a significant loss.

People who have specialized in the study of the grief process have observed that following the initial phase of condolences, caregivers tend to discontinue their support of the person suffering a loss. They point out that friends usually assume that, in a couple of weeks, the grieving person should be "getting on with life." In reality the grief process is more like a journey that should be expected to last no less than eighteen months to two years and as long as five years in the case of murder. I distinctly remember carefully marking each milestone along the way and feeling very encouraged to have made it one month, two months, six months, and a year.

The care and support given to me and my family during the weeks and months that followed our tragedy was so marvelous that it would make a good handbook on how to support the grieving. Our friends have continued to be present throughout our entire ordeal, which has become more like a saga. People have found meaningful and thoughtful ways to be supportive.

My needs were unique. I needed to see and be with people who were neither reporters nor associated with law enforcement. It gave me assurance that a normal life was still out there. Quite often special friends would just stop by for a visit, and sometimes one of them would even spend the night, which was probably somewhat uncomfortable for them because of all the police activity. Occasionally, unexpected flowers would be delivered, especially on dates that would have been an anniversary or birthday. Lots of notes and letters continued to come, and sweet treats were often brought, because all of my acquaintances know that I am a "dessert freak."

> *"There is a sort of invisible blanket between me and the world. I find it hard to take in what anyone says . . . Yet, I want the others to be about me. I dread the moments when the house is empty."*
> —C. S. LEWIS

My children's friends also continued to be very caring. Michelle's doctor surprised her one day by sending a beautiful catered meal from a very nice restaurant. One of Keith's friends in Kentucky sent a large gift basket called "Taste of Kentucky" containing such specialty items as Derby Pie. They also sent gifts for the grandsons, Scotty and Grant. These random acts of kindness came some time after the initial tragedy.

Caring for the wounded can also be done in much simpler ways than those just mentioned. The important thing about those deeds was that they came weeks and months after my husband's death. It has caused me to be keenly aware that giving care to those who have endured a significant loss should be ongoing. God meant for us to be caregivers. None of us ever expects to be on the receiving end of that care, but inevitably we will be. It is then that we will become fully cognizant of just how much we need people in our lives.

Isolation

One of the most common feelings that people seem to express during a time of adversity is the feeling of *isolation*. In his book, *A Grief Observed,* C. S. Lewis wrote, "There is a sort of invisible blanket between me and the world. I find it hard to take in what anyone says . . . Yet, I want the others to be about me. I dread the moments when the house is empty."

These were feelings that were a part of him when he was in deep grief because of the loss of his wife. He has such an excellent ability to describe human emotion. "An invisible blanket between himself and the world" portrays so clearly a part of what we often feel in a time of calamity, no matter what kind of calamity. It is almost as if no one else can quite be behind that "blanket" with you. Yet, in another sense, it is very important that others be there. As Lewis says, "I want others about me," even though, what they are saying may be a bit of a blur.

At some time you may have felt awkward and reluctant to go into a situation where there had been a serious calamity or crisis. Often people who would like to be comforters feel inadequate in such situations. They feel especially uncomfortable in the presence of the person suffering the tragedy. People dread this encounter because they just don't know what to say, and no one wants to say the *wrong* thing.

That fear is a relatively needless one. Notice what C. S. Lewis is saying in the passage above, "I find it hard to take in what anyone says." That, I believe, is true of most people in a crisis atmosphere. It was certainly true of me. Just remember, it's not the words you say when you come; it's that you came.

In our own tragedy, I doubt that I could tell you much of what was said to me, but I clearly remember being amazed that the hospital actually allowed so many people to be processed through tight security to the trauma floor. Also, I have a reasonably clear memory of the faces of those who were there, and if there are some that I don't remember, it's because there were so many that it was not possible to see them all. It's not the words you say when you come; it's that you are there!

Invest Yourself in People

To belong to the Lord means that we should reflect His spirit, which means that a Christian's nature should be that of a caregiver to the wounded. Caring about others is a trait that God meant for His people to either have or work very hard at developing. The Lord didn't intend that we turn inward and think only about "me and mine." In Philippians 2:4, we read, "Each of you should look not only to your own interests, but also to the interests of others."

Jesus modeled this trait for us all through His ministry as He invested Himself in people. We may tend to visualize Jesus as traveling about the countryside with a small, rag-tag band of followers, but that's not true. He seemed to constantly have a sizable entourage around Him. Luke 6:17 says, "A large crowd of his disciples was there and a great number of people from all over Judea, from Jerusalem, and from the coast of Tyre and Sidon who had come to hear him . . . ." Luke 8:19 says, "Now Jesus' mother and brothers came to see him, but they were not able to get near him because of the crowd."

Do you think that Jesus attracted people because He was handsome? The scriptures say that He had no earthly beauty or majesty. He certainly did not have a rock band, which is what seems to attract crowds today. Although there were some who came for ulterior motives, most people flocked to Jesus because He was willing to invest himself in them *personally.*

Investment in people doesn't come without cost, as Jesus found out. It costs time, inconvenience, energy, emotion, and maybe even some money, but it is an investment from which we get back at least as much as we put in, if not more.

> *Like yeast in bread dough, it is action, not just words, that makes the difference in our relationships.*

There are people who don't find it comfortable or convenient to spend much of their time with other people. Some go all through life without making any significant bonds with others. Some have kept themselves so separate that when any adversity strikes them personally, few feel close enough to help them. I have known people who became ill and had no one in their lives from whom they could expect help. Such a life must be empty indeed, and it probably comes about because that person was never willing to invest himself in others.

The Lord didn't intend that life be lived that way. The Word of God makes the message clear that we are to care about people. Like yeast in bread dough, it is *action,* not just words, that makes the difference in our relationships.

Share the Sorrow; Share the Joy

There will be times when you will be the one reaching out with kindness to someone, and just as certainly, there will be times when *you* will be the recipient. Ecclesiastes 4:9–10 is so true: "Two are better than one, because they have a good return for their work: If one falls down his friend can help him up. But pity the man who falls and has no one to help him up!" Everyone will have a time when he needs someone to build him up, pick him up, and perhaps hold him up for awhile.

Even in success, the joy is so much sweeter if there is someone with whom to share it, but in failure or in adversity, we really need someone who will give us encouragement. It's that "one another" factor that we see so generously sprinkled throughout God's Word. It might be just a little note, a knowing pat on the arm, or a smile, but sometimes it needs to be a lot more, and that might be when we become a bit reluctant.

> *In the Christian dispensation, a neighbor is anyone who needs our help—even our enemies.*

Nowhere in the Bible is that message more graphically illustrated than in the familiar story of the Good Samaritan in Luke 10. Sometimes, our reasoning is much too similar to that of the Jewish lawyer who asked, "And *who* is my neighbor?" The person next door? My best friends? Or just an acquaintance? Surely the Lord doesn't mean someone that I don't even know. Notice, the Jewish lawyer didn't want to waste his time where it wasn't required of him either.

The principle of "loving our neighbor" is not something that was begun in the New Testament. It was a commandment in the Old Testament given to the Israelites in Leviticus 19:18, but this principle, like so many others, was expanded in the New Testament era. The term "neighbor" became much more inclusive. Matthew 5:43 says, "You have heard that it was said, 'Love your neighbor and hate your enemy.' But I tell you: Love your enemies . . . ." In the Christian dispensation, a neighbor is anyone who needs our help—even our enemies.

Nature of a People-Person

Let us carefully examine the caring spirit of this man called "The Good Samaritan," and perhaps it will become more obvious what ingredients are "in the mix" when someone is truly a "people-person":

1. He stopped because of real compassion for another person. It would have been much easier for him to have followed the examples of the priest and the Levite. There was no obligation for him to stop, and it probably was not particularly convenient for him. Note those two words—"obligation" and "convenient." Those are two major factors as we decide whether or not to take action when we see a need before our very eyes. Sometimes we take action because of obligation, which is not a very noble motive, although it might be better than doing nothing. In fact, it has been my experience that once I'm involved with helping, "genuinely caring" comes quite naturally to me.

2. The Good Samaritan did not try to judge the worthiness of his recipient. Fortunately, God did not make us responsible for being able to accurately judge the worthiness of those who may

> *God did not charge us to see through people, but to see people through!*

need us on various occasions. In fact, He says that we may be *entertaining angels unaware.* The thing for which He *does* hold us responsible is serving others. God did not charge us to see through people, but to see people through!

3. The Good Samaritan helped when there was no reason to expect any accolades for his service. There seemed to be no witnesses. Human nature does not mind a pat on the back or maybe a plaque for meritorious service. It would likely do us good to practice doing more good deeds anonymously. How many of us would get down in the trenches and help the unlovable of this world, if no one knew? The Bible says that if we get all our praise here on earth, we may not have so much reward left when we get to heaven. The Good Samaritan could hardly expect any praise for what he did. The man he rescued might not even live. He might even be a Jew, who would normally not associate with a lowly Samaritan. He ministered for *no one* to see and without any reason to expect as much as a thank you.

   4. He was willing to interrupt his plans. He was obviously going somewhere for some purpose. He was delayed, inconvenienced, and probably lost sleep. We know that he spent some of his own money.

   I don't know about your time constraints, but my calendar gets to be quite sacred, with certain days and times allotted to various important things. I become uncomfortable when I see my schedule going awry. Now, isn't that just exactly when God lays an *opportunity* right in the middle of our road? Sometimes we are so obsessed with our own agenda

> *"As we have opportunity, let us do good."*
> —GALATIANS 6:10

that we could stumble over a hungry orphan on our way to a committee meeting on "How to Feed Hungry Orphans"! It's so obvious that God would have us put down our agendas and pick up the opportunity He put there for us.

   5. The Good Samaritan became personally involved. He didn't say, "Call me if I can help." He could see what needed to be done and probably didn't have his cellular phone to call 9-1-1. It meant getting his own hands dirty. He personally disinfected and bandaged that wounded man, and put him on his own donkey. He personally looked after him during the night. That kind of personal involvement is the kind that really allows the spirit of the Lord to shine through us.

Sometimes I wonder if the Samaritan ever saw the man that he helped again. If so, what was their relationship? I have observed that when people have gone through a crisis together, their bond of friendship really tightens. There really *is* always some *good* that sifts its way through the ashes of adversity and settles upon the bruised ones.

The Gift of Empathy

One of the advantages of having experienced tragedy first-hand is that you likely learn how to better relate to others in crisis. Today, I feel uniquely qualified to turn outward to those in adversity. It's not because I know new and clever things to say; it's because people who are suffering just see me walk in the room, and they know that I, too, have been where they are. There is an immediate bonding and mutual *empathy*.

> *I consider one of the pluses of having experienced tragedy to be the blessing of being better qualified to minister to the wounded.*

Empathy is something people can have only if they have been in a similar circumstance. Therefore, I consider one of the pluses of having experienced tragedy to be the blessing of empathy—being better qualified to minister to the wounded by feeling their wounds with them. However, I do find that now, as I walk through tragedy with others, it takes much more out of me. I feel really drained, and I think it's because of that deeper empathy that I feel.

My brother lost a teenage son to accidental drowning only about four months after Bob's death. My brother seemed to want my support above all others. For the reasons mentioned above, my words meant more to him; therefore, I tried to call and talk with him almost every day. That was so hard for me! I thought I would die! After every conversation, I felt ill and wondered, *Why is this so hard for me?* In years past, I had walked with others through tragedy.

Later, I heard a man telling a story about a degenerative disease that had taken the lives of all of his children. He is now helping other families whose children have that disease.

> *"Praise be to God . . . who comforts us in all our troubles, so that we can comfort those in any trouble with the comfort we ourselves have received from God."*

He said, "I just cry for those people who are losing their precious children to this disease."

The interviewer said, "You have such compassion!"

The man replied, "Yes, I do have very deep compassion for them, but I know that some of my tears are still for my own loss."

And I thought, *That's it!* That is really what makes deep and genuine empathy so special. Some of the emotion we feel for others is still for our own loss.

Nevertheless, one of the positives about having experienced significant loss is that it qualifies us, like nothing else, to be genuinely able to touch lives and encourage and influence others who need support in adversity. I know that God meant it to be that way.

One of my favorite passages has always been 2 Corinthians 1:4: "Praise be to the God and Father of our Lord Jesus Christ, the Father of compassion and the God of all comfort, who comforts us in all our troubles, so that we can comfort those in any trouble with the comfort we ourselves have received from God."

That passage lets us know that God's loving, caring spirit will be shown to us in times of trouble as He bathes us in comfort through the countless kindnesses and deeds of other people. Then, after we have been the recipient of such comfort, we should be equipped to bathe others with that same kindness. If we will do as this passage exhorts us to do, there should never be a shortage of comforters and caregivers, because, as surely as adversity comes, more comforters will be qualified through that process explained in 2 Corinthians 1:3–4.

As with all the traits that we have examined, the trait of being a caregiver is one that should be practiced long, long before you find yourself in need of comforters. When we have made it a way of life to turn outward and actively care for the wounded, not just our closest friends, but anywhere we see some need, we will be amazed at the storehouse of blessings and resources that will be ours when adversity strikes home.

What a Caregiver Learns

Let's bring into focus the specific ways that being a caregiver prepares us for our own future adversity:

1. What to expect with tragedy. When we have been through a number of crises with other people, we become experienced with tragedy and are not quite so overwhelmed when the crisis is our own. In a sense, we become seasoned veterans. We will have experienced a wide variety of problems and tragedies. I'm not at all suggesting that it's not more intense when it is personal, but having been there before with others helps to stabilize and strengthen our defenses. By walking through crises with others, we become more aware of the magnitude of disasters that can possibly befall us during the span of a lifetime. It's not possible to be close to those who are suffering without becoming very cognizant of the fact that it's quite possible, and even likely, that similar disasters can strike in our own families.

A number of years ago, I recall rushing to the hospital one weekend to be with a sweet young woman whose husband had suddenly suffered an almost fatal heart attack. Because it was a weekend, hardly anyone was aware or able to be there to help give support. I stayed with her all night and never left her side until sometime the next day when her relatives from out of town began to arrive. For many hours her husband's life hung in the balance.

That long period of hanging on the precipice with another person I now view as one of life's experiences that made me who I was at Parkland Hospital on March 3rd and 4th of 1994, as my own husband's life ebbed away. Certainly, I drew comfort and strength from that large crowd of supporters on that night, but somewhere in the mix was the fact that I had experienced this scenario several times before with other people. This time I was the one on the receiving end; and, somehow, even as intense and painful as the experience was, it was not completely foreign to me.

> *An interruption to our day may be something that God knows needs to have a higher priority.*

At the beginning of this book, it was mentioned that we are, to some degree, the sum total of all our life experiences. So, if we will "walk through the valley" with other people, it will be a part of who we are when it's our turn to make that walk.

2. By turning outward, serving, and ministering to other people, we are doing the Lord's work. The Lord works through those who are willing to serve others, and His Word repeatedly exhorts us to encourage one another. Hebrews 3:13 says, "Encourage one another daily." When Peter was being restored, he was told over and over by Jesus, in John 21:15, "Feed My sheep!" Other passages speak to us saying, "Build up one another" (1 Thessalonians 5:11) and "As often as you have done it unto one of these, you have done it unto me" (Matthew 25:40). If we have become too busy to do this, we definitely need to *re-prioritize*.

Jesus had only three years to complete His ministry, and yet He always seemed calm and relaxed, even under pressure. He accomplished what He could, and He fully concentrated on each opportunity as it arose. He trusted His calendar to God and re-routed things when necessary. We should learn to trust our day-to-day flow of events to God. An interruption to our day may be something that God knows needs to have a higher priority. It would help us to study Jesus as He calmly went His way, giving high priority to the wounded. When we do that, people are drawn, not to us, but to Jesus. When we reach out to other people, what they see in us is Jesus.

3. In reaching out to others, we experience the entire range of human responses to tragedy and crisis. We learn valuable lessons for ourselves in the process. We learn that there are no pat answers as to why these things happen, and we come to suspect that many of our natural, human responses in these situations are not particularly productive. It is in this area that genuine trust in God can really take root and grow. When we realize that there is no human response that will change the irreversible nature of the disaster, there comes a sense of overpowering helplessness.

It was in that kind of helplessness that Paul was told by the Lord in 2 Corinthians 1:9, "My power is made perfect in weakness." After digesting that statement, Paul said, "That is why for Christ's sake I delight in weaknesses, in insults, in hardships, in persecutions, in difficulties. For when I am weak, *then* I am *strong.*" When we really come to terms with our helplessness, we begin to realize that if we are to make it through adversity in life, it will be God, not us, who will see us through. We learn much about appropriate human response to adversity while ministering to the wounded.

> *When we help to carry the burdens of others, we soon realize that our own burdens are not so heavy after all.*

4. Turning outward to others will cause us to put our own problems in perspective. When we help to carry the burdens of others, we soon realize that our own burdens are not so heavy after all.

When my younger grandson was having one of his surgeries, our family was sitting in the surgery waiting room at Children's Hospital, feeling the normal amount of stress. We were soon to learn that a family sitting nearby had a baby girl in surgery for a brain tumor. Her surgery was their last hope, and the prognosis was not optimistic. Our burden suddenly began to feel like a feather compared to their pain. If you want to really get your problems in perspective, walk down the road with a few other sufferers.

5. Finally, actively *doing* something for someone who is hurting takes the focus off self. There is something therapeutic about *taking action* to minister to the needs of others.

The famous psychiatrist, Dr. Karl Meninger, was asked, "What would you do if you thought you were going crazy?"

He said, "I would go out and find someone less fortunate and *serve.*"

Dr. Maxwell Maltz said, "One of the most pleasant thoughts for any individual is the thought of being *needed*— that he is important enough to help another human being."

Dr. Laura Schlesinger was recently asked on her radio program how to help young children to work through the trauma of the kidnapping and murder of one of their classmates. Dr. Schlesinger urged that they help the children make pretty cards of encouragement for the parents of the victim. She said that by their *actively doing something* for someone involved in the case, it would cause these children to take the focus off themselves, off their own worries, grief, and fears. Not only would it take the focus off themselves, it would actually place that focus on someone else.

That is the same blessing that comes to any one of us, at any age, when we are willing to turn outward, because the focus is off self. The caregiver is never as conscious of his own problems. Perhaps having scrutinized some of the blessings that are ours when we prepare for adversity by caring for the wounded, we might find it more important to do so.

Turning outward does not mean that we choose a few close friends and minister only to them. It was Jesus who said in Matthew 5:46, "If you love those who love you, what reward will you get? Are not even the tax collectors doing that?" Jesus said that even people with no particular morals or principles will do that much. If we do that, we are not following the example that Jesus modeled for us. When we are so selective in our outreach, we are limiting ourselves and our experiences, and we are short-changing the Lord.

And It Will Be Given To You

Concerning ministering to others, Jesus also said in Luke 6:38, "Give and it will be given to you. A good measure, pressed down, shaken together and running over, will be poured into your lap." This passage is sometimes used when there is discussion of financial giving. However, in context, this passage is really talking more about relationships with people. If you really make the effort to become a people-person, you will see what this passage means. Actively serve, encourage and help people, and you will see the promise of this passage fulfilled in ways you cannot imagine! What we give has a way of coming back multiplied.

Life is a journey that was not meant to be traveled alone. When people start withdrawing themselves from others, they are in trouble. It has been said of Cain in the Genesis story of Cain and Abel, that by failing to be his brother's keeper, Cain failed to keep himself. I wonder if that isn't true of every person who fails to be his brother's keeper.

> *Jesus knew that our reaching out to others would not only bless those who are wounded, but would also prepare us for our own day of adversity.*

In a study at the University of California, a group headed by Lisa Berkman found that persons without strong ties to other people die at two to five times the rate of those who have strong social ties. This was true regardless of diet, exercise, smoking, and other factors.

And one Jewish rabbi said, "Anyone who travels too far alone goes mad." That comment reminds me that so often high-profile criminals are described as "loners."

I believe that the Lord made us need people, and that's why He knew that the church was necessary for us. He knew that our reaching out to others would not only bless those who are wounded, but would also prepare us for our own day of adversity. Like the Good Samaritan, Jesus saw us when we were strangers in the middle of His road. We must have looked a mess, but He stopped anyway. Now that His Spirit lives in us, we should desire to make a difference in the lives that we find along our roads.

*"Prepare your minds
for action;
be self-controlled."*

—

1 Peter 1:13

Widow recounts slaying

Murder trial opens in driveway holdup

By Steve Scott
Staff Writer of The Dallas Morning News

The driveway robber who fatally shot her husband last March didn't look like a killer, Pat Scott says.

She told jurors in state District Judge Larry Baraka's court Wednesday that when the young man strolled into the couple's garage, she thought for an instant he might be a neighbor or some other acquaintance. Nothing about his smooth skin and refined features suggested violence.

"He didn't look like someone who'd be about to rob you or kill you," Mrs. Scott said. "His clothing was nice, and he was nice-looking."

That illusion, she said, was quickly dispelled. Minutes later, 63-year-old Robert C. "Bob" Scott lay dying in the alley behind their home, a single bullet wound in his head.

Mrs. Scott recounted the March 3, 1994, robbery and shooting Wednesday afternoon for jurors in the capital murder trial of Derek Haggerty, 21.

She said she and her husband had just returned home about 8:30 p.m. after eating dinner out and running a few errands. She had just gotten out of their car when the man stepped into the garage, put her in a headlock and took her rings at gunpoint. Her husband, she said, ran into the alley to yell for help.

Mrs. Scott testified that the man then took her husband's jewelry. He charged Mr. Scott and opened fire in apparent rage after the magazine fell from his pistol, spilling some bullets across the driveway.

She testified that she later gave police a description of the attacker, which an artist used to draw a composite sketch. Mrs. Scott could not, however, positively identify Mr. Haggerty as her husband's killer.

Mr. Haggerty's defense attorney, Charles Maduka, focused attention on that and on Mrs. Scott's inability to choose Mr. Haggerty from a live police lineup. In it, she selected another man who she said more closely resembled the attacker.

Assistant District Attorney Jason January told jurors in an opening statement that he would present evidence showing that Mr. Haggerty bought the murder weapon — a .380-caliber semiautomatic pistol — several days before the killing. The gun was confiscated during Mr. Haggerty's arrest two weeks after the killing.

Mr. January said he would also show that Mr. Haggerty was involved in pawning several of Mrs. Scott's rings.

Mr. Scott was the first of two men killed early last year during holdups in their driveways. Michael McManemin, 39, was killed last March 14 outside his northwest Dallas home by a robber who stole his Rolex watch.

The gunman in that case, 21-year-old Wendell Lamont Pervis, was sentenced to life in prison last month on a capital murder charge.

CHAPTER

6

Self-Control
Steadies
the Vessel

WITHIN A FEW WEEKS following my husband's murder, arrests were being made. There had been two people involved. One had driven the pickup truck, and the other young man had been the shooter. The driver was arrested first and told the police everything. One of the things that he told the police was that the shooter had said that he was going to come back and "silence" me. For about two days the police hesitated about telling me that my life had been threatened. They were already giving me very good protection. Finally, the lead detective called and asked to come by for a visit.

The detective sat in the living room of my home about two o'clock that Tuesday afternoon and, with deliberate reserve, began to explain that my life had been threatened. He spoke so cautiously that I began to wonder if he thought I might explode in terror.

"Mrs. Scott, I didn't want to tell you this, but we think you may be in danger. We have just arrested the driver of the pickup truck in your case. He has told us that the shooter wants to come back and kill you."

God was still shielding me from the harsh reality of what I was being told. It was as if this ominous-sounding information were being said about someone else. I felt calm, but I knew that my son and daughter would *not* be calm.

The detective hastened to add, "We don't think that he would really try to get to you, but we must take all precautions. We are watching your house, but at the moment this guy is still on the loose. Hopefully, we will soon have him in jail."

Then he said that he would like to send a special detective to visit with me about what further precautions could be taken. There would be a number of new security measures.

As the detective was leaving, I remembered one quick errand that I needed to run; so, I got in the car and left. Apparently I still had not grasped the seriousness with which the police viewed this threat. Also, it was difficult to be so protected that I could not even run a simple errand.

Only moments after I left the house, the detective from the Security Division was at my front door. When I didn't answer the door, he became alarmed. He called all my family members in his effort to find me. When I got home from my brief errand, my telephone message recorder was filled with frantic calls from detectives and anxious family members. Feeling a bit embarrassed, I called everyone and assured them that I was fine. The people from the Security Division were back at my door within fifteen minutes! They went over my house inside and outside, making numerous recommendations for better security. Then they began going over security procedures for me personally to follow:

- Don't walk to the curb to pick up your morning newspaper.
- Sleep with the bedroom door locked, even though a police officer is in the next bedroom.
- On the night stand beside my bed there would at all times be a panic button, a pepper spray, a cellular telephone, and a flashlight.

- Special instructions were given about how to expedite entering and exiting the garage. This new way of life was to become my routine.

It seemed that I had two options: (1) I could let this threat become a reign of terror, which would consume me, or (2) I could take all the precautions and then leave it in God's hands. If the attacker was determined to kill me, he might just find a way. I chose to believe that he was not quite that desperate, but all the security was put in place. My house was probably the safest house in North Dallas.

The Need for Self-Control

God continued to give me just what was needed when it was needed. This time I needed self-control to steady the vessel in this worsening storm. I continued to sleep peacefully at night, and all that equipment on my night stand actually gave me confidence. Of course, that police officer in the next room was a courage-booster, too. Nevertheless, the trait of self-control was an indispensable tool throughout my ordeal.

William F. Buckley once said that heroism is the ability

> *When we read about great heroes of history, the one trait that they have in common is the virtue of self-control.*

to refrain from doing what is wrong and what one is tempted to do. Such a definition could well be applied to the subject of self-control. When we read about great heroes of history, the one trait that they have in common is the virtue of self-control.

One of the most notable examples of self-control comes from the harrowing stories about hikers who, while hiking in the woods, have had an encounter of the worst kind with a grizzly bear. The most common and natural response would be to run as fast as possible. Unfortunately, our most *natural* response to a crisis is not always the wisest one. People who are experienced in such matters as bear encounters say that the only appropriate response is to crouch face down, hands covering the back of the head, and lie very still, pretending to be dead. The bear may toss you about with its mighty paws. It may maul you, or even take a bite out of your back. Nevertheless, it is necessary for you to continue to play dead, or else you will be. Now, that's self-control!

Self-control is one of the most important traits to have in place during any crisis. It's important because, just as in the case of the encounter with the grizzly bear, the most natural thing to do or to think is not necessarily the most expedient. Therefore, the struggle will rage between the *natural* response to adversity and the more *expedient* response.

The scriptures speak often of self-control as a virtue that belongs in the character of a Christian. In Galatians 5:23, self-control is listed as part of the fruit of the Spirit. In 2 Peter 1:6, we read that in order to escape the corruption in this world caused by evil desires, we should "Make every effort to add to your faith goodness, and to your goodness knowledge, and to your knowledge *self-control,* and to self-control perseverance."

Reason vs. Passion

The Greek word used here for "self-control" is *egkrateia,* which means "reason fights against passion . . . and reason wins!" In Greek, the word recognizes human desires and passions, but those emotions are servants, not rulers. Literally, *egkrateia* means "the ability to take hold of one's self." The *King James Version* of the Bible interpreted *egkrateia* as "sober," but the *New International Version* translates it as "self-control."

The passage in 2 Peter 1:6 describes the growing process for a Christian. That passage causes us to recognize the need to continue gaining knowledge and developing certain traits and attitudes. It is possible that one's whole way of life may need some adjustment. Such change will not likely come easily.

Taking that difficulty into consideration, the Bible urges that self-control be added to Christian character. Just as a child learns which behaviors please or displease parents, so the Christian through the Word of God learns which behaviors please or displease the Father. Then comes the struggle to implement the pleasing behaviors. It's no wonder that self-control is the third trait listed in 1 Peter 1:6 and is mentioned so frequently in various other passages.

Paul spoke of his efforts of self-control in 1 Corinthians 9:26–27: "I do not run like a man running aimlessly; I do not fight like a man beating the air. No, I beat my body and make it my slave so that after I have preached to others, I myself will not be disqualified for the prize." Paul recognized the absolute necessity of our taking control of ourselves or risk losing our souls. Self-control requires a conscious effort. In fact, Paul makes it sound like an athlete who is in training for something very important.

Some passages, such as Titus 2:2, Titus 2:5 and Titus 2:12, use a different Greek word to give a slight shade of difference in meaning to the word "self-control." The word used is *sophrosane*, which means "sensible, temperate, or governing our own instincts." Plato called it "mastery of self." This is the same Greek word used in 1 Peter 1:13, the theme passage for this book. That passage says, "Prepare your minds for action; be self-controlled."

William Barclay says that Peter is actually saying, "Gird up the loins of your mind." The men of the East wore long flowing robes. All that extra fabric would get in their way when they engaged in strenuous activity. Therefore, they would roll up some of the fabric and tuck it under a wide belt which they wore at the waist. The idea in this passage is that when our faith has not been tested, it will have *excesses,* which get in the way. Peter is urging us to get rid of the excesses and focus on who we are and what our destination is. Only then will our faith be strong enough to withstand the adversity we will surely face.

Seeing Life with Sanity

After telling them to "prepare their minds," Peter said, "Be self-controlled"—*sophronein*—sensible or sane. A person who is "sane" is usually considered to be so for several reasons. One measure of sanity is seeing things in proper perspective. We are able to distinguish between what is really important and what is not. Sane people will not be prone to run out of control with unbalanced fanaticism, nor do they tend to be unrealistically indifferent to what goes on around them.

> *It is only when God is given His proper place that everything else takes its proper place.*

Now we can understand the depth of this word as it is used in the passage of 1 Peter 1:13. It is only when we can see the affairs of this world in the light of eternity that we can put them in proper (mentally sane) perspective. It is only when God is given His proper place that everything else takes its proper place. Barclay says, "This does not mean that the Christian is to be lost in gloomy joylessness, but it *does* mean that his approach to life must not be frivolous and irresponsible. To take matters seriously is to be *aware* of their real importance and to be ever mindful of their consequences in time and eternity."

Will You or Won't You?

Sinful tendencies and desires of the flesh still war with the Holy Spirit within the Christian. A mere law against such tendencies would not control such desires. It requires the participation and the will of the individual Christian. The will of the individual is where the role of self-control becomes glaringly apparent. It is when the human will wars on the side of the Holy Spirit that the fleshly desires can be held in check; i.e., self-control.

When you decide to build traits that will serve you well in a future day of adversity, you will of necessity consider the virtue of self-control. The other traits discussed in this book could hardly be developed without a strong degree of self-control. You have to decide that you *will* have self-control . . . or you *won't*.

Unhealthy attitudes and unholy desires can come to us without having been invited or nurtured. Feelings of resentment and anger seem to be able to sprout without our consciously bidding them welcome. Even our seemingly normal passions, emotions, and feelings require our diligence to keep them in check. The fact is, God calls His people to a higher way of thinking and behaving, a way that does not come naturally—the way of self-control. Self-control is a vital ingredient as we try to implement a style of thinking and behaving that reflects Jesus and brings Him glory.

> *God calls His people to a higher way of thinking and behaving, a way that does not come naturally—the way of self-control.*

Teaching Self-Control

Self-control is a virtue that evolves through a learning process. It is interesting to watch parents trying to teach self-control to their young children. For example, when a grandparent visits, the children usually have come to expect a "surprise" or gift, but the parents have said, "Don't ask!" The poor little ones are literally squirming with desire to ask the grandparent if there is a present, and the adult talk seems to go on for an eternity before the time finally comes for bestowing gifts. Rare is the child who has mastered the self-control to avoid broaching the subject. And out bursts, "Grandpa, what did you bring me?"

Taming Temper Tantrums

Children also go through the process of learning that angry outbursts are not appropriate behavior. Some never learn it and grow to adulthood with an uncontrolled temper. Some people are described as "having a temper." Perhaps it would be more appropriate to say, "That person does not *control* his or her temper."

Controlling anger is one important aspect of self-control. Probably one of the most unbecoming behaviors in a Christian is exhibiting outbursts of anger or uncontrolled temper. Paul wrote in Colossians 3:8: "But now rid yourselves of all such things as these: *anger,* rage, malice, slander, and filthy language from your lips." Almost every word in that sentence is closely associated with out-of-control anger.

Many people say that they absolutely cannot control their tempers. That usually means that they didn't grow up being taught to control their tempers. People who have grown to adulthood without learning to discipline themselves in this regard will surely have a great struggle mastering control of angry outbursts of temper. Yet, I have witnessed some absolutely amazing transformations in people who seriously make the effort to become Christlike.

As soon as I say "Christlike," someone will invariably say, "But Jesus drove the moneychangers out of the temple." Let me urge you to carefully read that passage in John 2:12–17. Does that passage say that Jesus' anger was out of control? I don't believe that He was ever out of control. Jesus made a very deliberate response to the blasphemy of God's temple. He deliberately wove a whip out of cords. This is not the action of a man in a fit of temper. Although Jesus spoke harshly to the Pharisees about their hypocrisy, He was certainly not characterized as a man who didn't control His temper.

On the contrary, Jesus described himself as being "meek and gentle" (Matthew 11:29). When Peter wrote of Jesus in 1 Peter 2:23, he said, "When they hurled insults at him, he did not retaliate; when he suffered, he made no threats." That describes a very controlled person. If we are to emulate Jesus, we must try to exercise self-control in situations when unkind or inconsiderate behavior is displayed toward us. That kind of behavior sets the Christian apart from the world.

> *"Do not make friends with a hot tempered man; do not associate with one easily angered."*

Proverbs 29:11 says, "A fool gives full vent to his anger." Even stronger than that is the passage in Proverbs 22:24: "Do not make friends with a hot tempered man; do not associate with one easily angered." As we gain knowledge from God's Word, we learn that the Lord wants His people to control reactions to feelings of anger and hostility.

Thought Control

Not only do we Christians need to control our outward behavior, but the Lord wants us to exercise self-control in the way that we *think*. Paul writes in 2 Corinthians 10:5, "Take captive every thought to make it obedient to Christ." We are even exhorted this way in Philippians 2:5: "Your attitude should be the same as that of Christ." It would be a worthy exercise to monitor our own thoughts and ask ourselves whether there is any similarity between our thinking and that of Christ.

If some person harms you by words or deeds, hurts your feelings, deceives you or threatens you, can you pause and ask yourself, *What would Jesus do in this situation? What would He think? What would He say?* The Bible is replete with examples of what Jesus would do.

There is a level of subconscious thinking for us, and sometimes sinful thoughts flutter through our minds. It's difficult to get a handle on such *subconscious* thoughts. However, if those thoughts stay more than a fleeting second, they become *conscious* thoughts, and we *can* and *should* be able to get a handle on them and throw them out!

> *It's so important to exercise self-control in our thinking, because our thoughts have a way of becoming spoken words and live actions.*

Marshall Keeble, a well known minister, used to say, "We may not be able to keep the birds from flying over our heads, but we don't have to allow them to make nests in our hair." It's so important to exercise self-control in our thinking, because our thoughts have a way of becoming spoken words and live actions.

The writer of Matthew 12:34 said, "Out of the overflow of the heart the mouth speaks." It is tempting to allow yourself sinful thoughts, because they are so private. No one else knows what's going on in your mind. Sometimes people just remove the self-control knob and think mean, judgmental thoughts. But ask yourself this question: *Who will I be, if I give free rein to such thinking?* You will be a person who tries to act one way in public, but in private, you are someone else. Jesus called these people hypocrites. Sooner or later that hidden person will emerge, perhaps in small ways and in unbecoming comments. What we think in the privacy of our own hearts is what we become.

> *"The greatest discovery in our generation is that human beings, by changing inner attitudes of their minds, can change all the outer aspects of their lives."*

William James, a Harvard psychologist, said, "The greatest discovery in our generation is that human beings, by changing inner attitudes of their minds, can change all the outer aspects of their lives." Such a formula has great significance for us in striving to live the Christian life.

Desire Control

Self-control needs to be our constant exercise, because Satan is always present and ready to tempt us at every opportunity (see 1 Peter 5:8). It was Satan who asked God to allow him to put Job to the test in Job 1:9–10. Satan apparently also asked the Lord to allow him to put Peter to the test. In Luke 22:31, Luke records these words of Jesus: "Simon, Simon, Satan has asked to sift you as wheat." Satan finds many ways to put God's people to the test.

Therefore, Christians must guard their desires, impulses, reactions to feelings, and attitudes. Satan knows which things we desire so much that we might be tempted to compromise our principles. James 1:14–15 tells us that "Each one is tempted when, by his own evil desire, he is dragged away and enticed. Then, after desire has conceived, it gives birth to sin."

Human beings want many things. We want wealth, diamonds, and a Mercedes. We want power and attention. Those things might not be wrong in themselves, unless we have to sacrifice our souls to get them. We have daily opportunities to practice our self-control over our desires.

In 1 Samuel 15 the account of King Saul's destruction of the Amalekites is given. God told him to completely destroy everything—take nothing. But Saul saw some fine-looking animals. He desired them. Unfortunately, Saul had not been in the habit of controlling his desires. Self-control was not a trait for which he was known. So, he took some of those fine animals, and when Samuel came to tell him of God's displeasure, Saul said that he had intended to sacrifice the animals to God. Samuel replied with these famous words: "To obey is better than sacrifice."

> *"If anyone considers himself to be religious and yet does not keep a tight rein on his tongue, he deceives himself, and his religion is worthless."*

Just as Saul's desires were out of control, it's quite possible for our own desires to be out of control. Many desirable things are put before us every day, and we often think that we want them. We must practice self-control, lest we, like Saul, find ourselves gratifying our own wishes above the will of God.

Tongue Control

There are so many areas of life that require our best efforts of self-control. However, the one which usually proves to be the most troublesome is the tongue. James 1:26 says, "If anyone considers himself to be religious and yet does not keep a tight rein on his tongue, he deceives himself, and his religion is worthless." Interestingly enough, James goes on to say in James 3:8, "But no man can tame the tongue. It is a restless evil full of deadly poison."

This passage sounds as if our speech is the most difficult area of self-control, and I agree that it is. People—even Christians—tend to tell unfavorable things about others when it's not necessary to do so. Part of disciplining ourselves to be more pleasing to God is to make a serious and sincere effort to control what we say. Since people speak approximately 25,000 words a day, we have ample opportunity to practice self-control in this area. Probably the very best way to exercise self-control over our speech is to practice listening more and speaking less.

What does the trait of self-control have to do with people who find themselves in the midst of crisis, tragedy, or any kind of adversity? Like all the other traits discussed in this book, self-control will serve you more effectively if it is already in place *before* the crisis occurs.

Mind Games

First, we should realize that the mind can play a myriad of games with us when we grieve or suffer adversity.

What if . . . ? Almost immediately, and certainly without any conscious effort, the mind begins thinking of scenarios in which this tragedy would not have occurred. I personally struggled with this one. I sometimes found myself thinking of things that might have changed the outcome of our tragedy. For instance, what if we had not gone directly home when we noticed the pickup following us?

If such thinking is out of control, people will even lie awake at night thinking of all the possibilities for a more favorable outcome. Such thoughts are not at all productive and will change nothing. If we have always practiced controlling the way we think, we will be much more successful in reining in unproductive, irrational thoughts.

Ascribe our feelings to the lost one. In cases where there has been a death, we sometimes mentally ascribe our own feelings of loss and loneliness to the one who has died. We have the illusion that our loved one is out there somewhere longing to be back with us. Such thinking causes us double grief—our own and the imagined grief of our loved one. If we have practiced taking control of our thinking, we will coax ourselves away from that kind of imaginary exercise and accept the fact that the "longing" is our own.

Self-pity. Another thinking problem in the face of adversity is that of self-pity. Quite easily, we can imagine that our own problem or catastrophe is worse than all others known to people. We may even dissolve into hopelessness and helplessness. In more rational moments, we know that such thinking is false. In fact, we need not look very far to find others with worse disasters than our own, such as in a hospital. Usually, though, it's only the person exercising self-control who makes the effort to look at the enormous suffering of others instead of just their own. It's controlled thinking that allows us to believe that life will go on for us and that there are still many hopeful possibilities for us to have a productive life.

General Dwight Eisenhower was once asked what would have happened during World War II if his invasion troops had been pushed back into the sea. He said, "It would have been very bad, but I never allow my mind to think in that way."

During my own tragedy, I let Bible messages saturate my mind. I thought of who God is and of His power and wisdom. Especially, I remembered the things that God had said to Job in chapters 38 through 41. Those words caused me not to even feel the need to say or think any of the things that Job had said. God had already spoken, saying that *He is in charge.*

Irrational and unproductive thinking are absolutely normal in times of crisis, but our healing depends on our ability to get past that kind of thinking. It is the trait of self-control that can come to our aid, allowing us to move beyond unproductive mental exercises.

Behavior Control

A lady spoke recently of a time when she suffered public humiliation, private disappointment, and pain because her son had been rebellious. He had behaved in ways unbecoming of his upbringing. She told of crying bitter tears, praying, and asking her friends to pray. She lost her appetite, could not sleep, and became ill. She said that she had not at all been prepared for such a disaster.

Then she said something that really caught my attention: "The next time some disaster comes my way, I will handle it much better!" And she *will* handle it much better, primarily because she has *decided* that she will handle it better. She realized that out-of-control behavior doesn't help anything.

The Greeks had a word which meant just the opposite of self-control—*akolasia.* It described a condition in which a person allowed his passion, lust, or emotions to be in complete control of his actions. They had another word, *akrasia,* which meant that reason or judgment fights, but passion wins.

Most of us find that we can identify with that second word. We know that it's more reasonable and sane to exercise self-control, but we sometimes lose the battle to our fleshly natures. Self-control is like a leg muscle. If the leg is immobilized in a cast, the muscle will weaken from lack of use. Then, when the cast is removed, and that leg muscle is really needed, it's too weak to function properly.

Get a Grip!

If our self-control is not used often enough, it will be too weak to help us overcome the tough hurdles we face from time to time. When unstable thoughts run rampant over our reason, we may, indeed, suffer more than necessary. Self-control is deeply involved with the mental process. If our self-control is in good condition, we are able to harness our thoughts and drive them in the direction that they should go.

> *Like a city whose walls are broken down is a person who lacks self-control.*
> —PROVERBS 25:28

We have to get a grip on our self-control. When there is fear, we guide our thoughts and emotions toward safety. When there is insecurity, we guide them toward shelter. When we feel collapse is near, we force those thoughts toward strength. Notice those three words: safety, shelter, and strength. All three are found only in one place—in the Lord. Self-control is the trait that can keep our focus on that truth!

> *Like a city whose walls are broken down*
> *is a person who lacks self-control.*
> Proverbs 25:28

"The testing of your faith develops perseverance."

—

JAMES 1:3

Bail is rejected for suspect in driveway robbery-slaying

By Steve Scott
Staff Writer of The Dallas Morning News

A capital murder suspect in the March 3 driveway robbery of a Far North Dallas man was ordered held without bail Friday after testimony that the suspect told a friend that he planned to return and kill the victim's widow.

During a preliminary hearing for Derek Haggerty, 20, a homicide detective testified that Dallas police have evidence that Mr. Haggerty pawned four of the widow's stolen rings the day after the killing.

Investigators also believe that a handgun seized during Mr. Haggerty's arrest earlier this month was used to kill retired bank executive Bob Scott, Detective D.A. Watts testified.

Mr. Scott, 63, was shot once in the head as he struggled with a robber outside the garage of his home in the 5700 block of En'Core Drive. Pat Scott, 58, Mr. Scott's wife, was robbed of jewelry at gunpoint but escaped unharmed.

The robbery was among more than two dozen similar holdups since January, most in North and Far North Dallas.

During Friday's hearing, Detective Watts said that Rickie Beasley, 26, a friend of Mr. Haggerty's who police say joined in several of the driveway robberies, **Please see BAIL on Page 32A.**

7

Only the Tenacious Survive

AS THE Dallas Police Department worked unrelentingly to arrest the man who actually pulled the trigger on the evening of March 3, 1994, our family could only wait for day-to-day progress reports. Finally, the detective called to say that they had made the arrest and to advise me to expect increased press coverage again.

The person arrested was a twenty-year-old, African-American man named Derek Haggerty, a football player who had dropped out of school. Ironically, while he was being interrogated at the police station, my daughter and I happened to be there to identify some of my jewelry that had been recovered.

We would later learn that, while we were at the police station, the murderer actually tried to make a daring escape from the interrogation room. While detectives were out of the room, Derek removed some acoustical tiles from the ceiling and tried to escape through the crawl space. Fortunately, they caught him before he could get away.

Soon Derek was indicted for my husband's murder. Newspapers carried pictures of him glaring angrily at reporters. His indictment didn't mean that life would return to normal for me. It only meant a new phase of our tragedy was beginning.

It meant that the Dallas Police Department would no longer be in charge of the case. I would now be meeting with prosecutors and investigators from the District Attorney's office. It was necessary then to walk the prosecution team through the crime scenario again and again. Every minute detail would be ferreted out and examined in preparation for the trial. The reliability of my testimony would hinge on the accuracy of these details.

I dreaded the thought of going through a trial; so I tried to think of it as something in the distant future. I actually blocked the prospect of the trial from my mind, except when the prosecution team came for their visits.

At this point, the thing that made me most proud and happy was to observe the resilience of my two children. They had been strong and supportive throughout this tragedy, and it pleased me to see them resuming their lives normally.

Michelle took little Scotty to a child psychologist to be sure that he was healing emotionally. He missed his grandfather dreadfully and constantly asked questions. The psychologist gave assurance that he would be fine and urged us to answer his questions openly.

Michelle had been in the process of preparing to enter medical school when our tragedy occurred. She had felt like throwing it all away but persevered and was accepted into medical school.

Keith returned to his work in Louisville, Kentucky, and he made frequent visits home to support and encourage me.

Tenacity Tested

Tenacity is a trait that all parents want for their children. This storm had severely tested that trait, and I felt blessed to see it alive and well in both my children.

Recently, I heard a man on the radio discussing a new business that he and his wife were trying to establish. The conversation sounded much like that of any budding entrepreneur, except for one thing. This man was a quadriplegic! He only casually mentioned that fact in the conversation. A quadriplegic is one who has no use of his hands, arms, legs, or feet, which means that he can't even do such ordinary things as bathe himself or brush his own teeth.

We might expect this man to live in helpless despair and bitterness. Not so! Since his disabling accident, he had been using his mental abilities to plan a way to produce an income for himself and his family. The attitude of that man epitomizes the trait of tenacity.

> *When we are endowed with the buoyancy of tenacity, we are like air-filled rafts on water; we will not sink!*

As we prepare ourselves for any kind of adversity, we definitely want to work toward becoming more resilient, tenacious people—buoyant people. When we are endowed with the buoyancy of tenacity, we are like air-filled rafts on water; we will not sink!

In our world where we are vulnerable to virtually any kind of disaster, it's so important to develop resilience. So many of us faced with the helplessness of becoming a quadriplegic would lose all hope. Many of us would likely spend all our energy to fuel our anger and bitterness, because such a fate had been dealt us. We would probably apply for government assistance.

It is doubtful that any of us know our own degree of buoyancy in stormy waters, until we actually come face to face with it. Of course, some storms are harder to survive than others, but no storms are survived without tenacity.

Becoming Elastic People

Let's first examine the meaning of the words used to define the kind of person who weathers a storm without being defeated.

Resilient. I have already mentioned the adjective "resilient," which means "one who recovers his strength, spirits, and good humor in a timely manner." According to Webster's dictionary, the term "resilient" originally was applied to something like elastic which would spring back quickly after being stretched. This helps us to better understand what the trait of resiliency does for the person whose endurance has been stretched to the limit.

Other adjectives, such as "tenacious" and "buoyant," are similar to "resilient," but there are shades of difference in their meanings.

Tenacious. "Tenacious" means "persistent and stubborn—one who holds firmly to something."

Buoyant. "Buoyant" refers to something that "will not sink."

Perseverance. The term most often used in the Bible to describe a buoyant person is "perseverance." It means "to pursue steadily any design or course, once begun." It's a trait that God wants us all to develop.

> *How could I quit when God was working so mightily on my side?*

As with most other traits, the trait of tenacity or perseverance comes more easily for some people than for others. Some traits almost seem to be innate or genetic. In my own life, I feel sure that being tenacious is an inherited trait. Both of my parents would have clawed a living out of the earth if it were necessary. They were definitely survivors, and they were quick to recognize that same trait in their firstborn—me. They repeatedly told the story of my first day of school.

It seems that I was so excited that I got dressed early and went outside to await the arrival of the school bus. However, the school bus driver, not realizing that I was old enough to go to school, whisked past our house without seeing that first grader so eagerly waiting. Horrified, I began running down the road chasing the school bus. I suppose that it never occurred to me that I couldn't catch that bus. I just continued running, until my parents finally came in the car and caught me. On that day, they knew for sure that their little first grader was endowed with perseverance.

Many years passed before that trait was tested in a really major storm of life. I will never forget, nor do I want to forget, the helplessness and total dependence on God that I experienced as the reality of Bob's murder made its way into my senses. I want to keep that memory, because, in that helplessness, I suddenly felt enveloped in God's love in a way that I had never before experienced.

It reminded me of the familiar hymn, *O Love That Will Not Let Me Go.* There truly was no place else to go. It was His love that gently nudged me onward, one day at a time. God never wants His people to quit or sink into despair and fear. In what seemed to be a wonderful gift, God took away fear and replaced it with perfect peace. How could I quit when God was working so mightily on my side?

Never a Quitter Be

Like someone whose boat was about to capsize in a storm, I was straining to see the safety of land. I wanted to see a time when life would be, at least, somewhat normal and meaningful again. I wondered what kind of life I could expect when the dark days of detectives, prosecutors, and media coverage subsided. Who would I be then?

I would no longer be a *wife*. Once or twice I had already heard people call me the "w" word. I had flinched at the sound of the word "widow." I didn't feel comfortable being described as a widow, but in reality, it was the appropriate term. Mentally, I asked myself if "widow" was who I would be now. From somewhere deep within my reserves, the answer came: *That term will have little to do with who you will be.* I believe that little voice inside me was the voice of perseverance poised to push me forward toward building a new and productive life.

A productive life glorifies God in some way. Philippians 2:13 makes us aware that people are the vehicles God uses to work His divine purposes: "For it is God who works in you to will and act according to his good purpose." Interestingly enough, throughout the ages, God always seemed to be able to work through people who had qualified in the school of adversity and failure. These were ordinary people, but they possessed the traits of resilience and tenacity. They were people who were not willing to be defeated by their circumstances. They were useful in God's plan, not because of their great abilities, but because they would not *quit*.

> *Peter rose tenaciously out of the ashes of despair to be one of the most powerful leaders in the early church.*

Abraham allowed Sarah to persuade him to take matters into his own hands. In trying to help God fulfill His promise to perpetuate a nation through his seed, Abraham gave the world Ishmael. But Ishmael was *not* the promised seed. It was only after Abraham had suffered great heartache and failure over this mistake that God was finally able to work His purposes through Abraham. What if Abraham had quit after that fiasco? As he walked with God, Abraham experienced pain and disappointment often. God tested his faith severely, yet Abraham held on obediently and tenaciously.

Jacob had some troublesome character traits, but he also had perseverance. We might almost wonder why God chose him. Jacob deceived his father and stole his brother's birthright. He had to flee his homeland and spent many years of heartache in exile. His life was filled with turmoil, and he even had a power struggle with God. Yet, Jacob had one trait that allowed God to work through him—tenacity! Though he stumbled so often, he never quit walking.

David, whose life was filled with bloody wars, committed adultery and murder. His children brought him grief and pain. What a failure. What despair. Many people would have turned away from God's service, feeling unworthy to even try to be God's instrument. Not David! He remained fiercely loyal to God, and God was able to use him mightily.

Peter. Perhaps no one has found himself at such a low ebb as the apostle Peter. After feeling so certain that his faith was strong, he found himself overcome by fear and denied Christ three times on the night that Jesus was arrested. Peter was so ashamed and disappointed in his failure that he wept bitterly. He had failed the Christ. Jesus had earlier told Peter, "Satan has asked to sift you, but I have prayed for you" (Luke 22:31). And Peter rose tenaciously out of the ashes of despair to be one of the most powerful leaders in the early church.

Perhaps we are better qualified after the school of adversity, pain and failure, because in that school we realize just how incapable and powerless we really are without God. These people all had one ingredient in common in their characters—they were not quitters.

Where's the Limit?

We all tend to wonder, though, what our own personal limit is when it comes to enduring adversity. We usually don't know where the limit is beyond which we could no longer persevere. However, God knows, and He made a very important promise in regard to "limits." The apostle Paul wrote about it in 1 Corinthians 10:13: "No temptation has seized you except what is common to man. And God is faithful. He will not let you be tempted beyond what you can bear."

A scholar, William Barclay, says that the Greek word translated "temptation" in this passage more closely means "test." It is something designed, not to make us fall, but to test us, so that we emerge from it stronger than ever," like glass tempered by fire. Any kind of adversity can really put us to the test.

However, the point of this passage is that others have experienced problems, tragedy and crisis just like yours, and they have been able to endure with God's help. Yet, there have always been those who either could not or would not persevere through difficult times. The history of the Hebrew people of the Old Testament shows a lack of tenacity and resilience in people.

Rest and Food

Even the outstanding character Elijah once thought that he had reached his personal limit. His story is told in 1 Kings 18 and 19. God had so mightily worked through him to defeat the prophets of Baal on Mt. Carmel. Then, when Jezebel threatened his life for having destroyed her prophets, Elijah ran for his life. He finally sat down under a tree and prayed to die. He said to God, "I have had enough, Lord."

In that statement, Elijah perfectly expressed how we feel when we are ready to quit. When we decide that we have reached our personal limits, we say to ourselves, to God, and to all who are in our realm of influence, "I've had enough!" That sentiment represents a decision made somewhere in the recesses of our hearts. It doesn't necessarily mean that there are absolutely no reserves left, and it doesn't mean that God can't pick us up and infuse us with new strength.

People today often find themselves in the same condition as Elijah—physically exhausted. His exhaustion weakened his resolve to fight on, which is precisely the culprit that causes us to want to quit. Elijah was tired of the struggle, emotionally and physically, and he decided that he was ready to quit.

> *Food and rest may make the difference in our ability to rise above the adversity threatening to defeat us.*

We need to be especially cognizant of the remedy that God prescribed for Elijah. God knew that Elijah was in need of nourishment and rest. He told Elijah to eat, drink some water, and rest. Then he ate, drank water, and rested a second time . . . and then a third time before going on to Horeb.

During a time of serious trouble, we frequently don't feel like eating, and sometimes we're not able to sleep well. Those two factors definitely affect our resilience and tenacity. Even those of us who normally persevere may find ourselves weakened with exhaustion, caused by failing to eat and sleep adequately.

It may sound trite, but when storms swirl about us, we must not forget to eat, even though we may not relish food. We must be sure to get adequate sleep also. It was God's prescription, and He is the Great Physician. If we are unable to sleep, we should see a doctor who can help. Food and rest may make the difference in our ability to rise above the adversity threatening to defeat us.

Exhaustion confuses our thinking, causing the situation to seem more hopeless than it is. That's what happened to Elijah in 1 Kings 19:10ff; his thinking had taken a downward spiral: "I have been very zealous for the Lord Almighty. The Israelites have rejected your covenant, broken down your altars, and put your people to death with the sword. I am the only one left. Now they are trying to kill me too."

When we're ready to quit, we often see our circumstances as hopeless, just as Elijah did. Elijah was mistaken, and God corrected him in 1 Kings 19:18: "Yet, I reserve 7,000 in Israel, all whose knees have not bowed down to Baal and whose mouths have not kissed him." In his exhaustion, Elijah had begun to feel alone in his struggle—a feeling that commonly overtakes those in the midst of adversity. In reality, he was far from alone; besides the 7,000 other Israelites, God was still there too!

> *"Those who hope in the Lord will renew their strength."*

Elijah may have been ready to give up on God, but God was not ready to give up on Elijah. When we're ready to quit, we're not interested in putting together a plan of action for moving forward. The last thing on Elijah's mind was making a plan of action, but God had a plan for him. He always has a plan for us, too, if we just refuse to quit.

Hope Helps

Most of us will, at some time, face circumstances of pain, loss, and disaster that we cannot repair. It's a fact of life that we are often completely powerless to put things back together as they once were. It's our hope in the Lord that gives us resilience. Isaiah said it best in Isaiah 40:31, "But those who hope in the Lord will renew their strength." It is unfortunate when we despair so much that we withdraw from that hope. We may begin to believe that life is unfair, but the Lord did not promise that life would be fair. Our judgment about fairness can cause us serious *faith failure*.

In Psalm 73:13 Asaph spoke of a time when he almost experienced faith failure because he was making a judgment about the fairness of life: "Surely in vain I have kept my heart pure. In vain I have washed my hands in innocence." He was thinking that, despite his faithfulness, God had allowed bad things to happen to him. In verse 14 he said, "All day long I have been plagued; I have been punished every morning." These are the very feelings that cause people to lose their faith and become quitters when serious adversity befalls them.

In an earlier passage in Psalm 73, Asaph had said, "But as for me, my feet had almost slipped. I had nearly lost my foothold." His feet were slipping, because he had a distorted perspective about his adversity. He could not see the big picture; he could only see the present. And what did he see? He saw the same thing that many of us see—people breaking all the rules and appearing to get away with it. There seemed to be no stigma attached to their ungodly behavior.

In fact, in today's society, such people may even get a lot of attention and glory. In Asaph's view, even God was blessing the wicked. Of course, scripture does say that "God sends rain on the just and the unjust" (Matthew 5:45). Asaph, like many people today, felt qualified to make a judgment about the fairness of such actions of God, and it damaged both his faith and his resilience.

Asaph finally regained his perspective, and in Psalm 73:16–17, he said, "When I tried to understand all this, it was oppressive to me, till I entered the sanctuary of God; then I understood their (the disobedient) final destiny."

Not unlike people of today, Asaph had probably put some distance between himself and God—possibly not reading the Word or praying much. So, when trouble came, he didn't have the tools with which to be resilient and hold fast to his faith. It was only when he drew close to God, that his perspective improved. Only then did he realize that, although the wicked looked as if they had it all, their *final* destiny was yet to be determined.

Then, in verse 21, Asaph felt penitent that he had allowed himself to think about God in such a perverse way: "When my heart was grieved and my spirit embittered, I was senseless and ignorant. I was a brute beast." This penitent spirit of Asaph was very similar to that of Job after his faith struggle during his time of adversity. In Job 42:3, Job said, "Surely I spoke things I did not understand, things too wonderful for me to know." And in verse 6 he said, "Therefore, I despise myself and repent in dust and ashes."

> *"And afterward you will take me into glory."*

The Reward of Repentance

A golden lesson emerges for us from these two penitent men. They both repented in deep anguish and sorrow for having blamed God for their adversity. Yet, their penitence came *before* any improvement in their physical circumstances. Their adversity had not gone away at this point. They became penitent, not because God had taken away their problems, but because they had become aware of *who their God was.* Suddenly, they were caused to realize that, no matter what happens in this small expanse of time called life, God is in control, and He loves His people.

Asaph concluded in Psalm 73:24, "You guide me with your counsel." The Word of God is our counsel and will keep us on the right track when we are dealing with life's problems. And, then, Asaph concluded, "And afterward you will take me into glory." That's the same promise that we hold dear as we struggle through pain and hardship in life. We must not allow ourselves to be lured into the devil's trap by quitting the race before we get to the finish line. We must develop perseverance for our times of adversity.

An Overcoming Spirit

Our creator believed perseverance to be a trait that His people needed to nurture. In numerous ways throughout scripture, He exhorted us to have this trait. However, a familiar mind-set today is the attitude that hardship is not deserved. Rather than working through adversity with determination, some people blame their problems on everyone and everything, from their upbringing to the Lord himself.

In contrast to that attitude, an elderly gentleman who had lived to be a hundred years old was asked how he had managed to get an education and become a respected attorney. He had come from a rather humble background to achieve great success.

The interviewer asked him, "Why do you think it is that so many of this country's great men have come from adverse and difficult backgrounds?"

The gentleman replied, "Those men achieved because it was necessary for them to overcome certain disadvantages."

People who survive adversity, pain, and hardship become stronger from the experience.

Paul praised the church in Thessalonica for its endurance. Early Christians had to overcome much hardship and persecution. Today we wonder how many would even come to worship if the air conditioning were not working. It may be that life has become so soft that few of us are willing to view tenacity, resilience, or perseverance as desirable traits. Today, mere inconvenience is equated with hardship.

In some cases people don't have the tenacity to hold fast when the outside community disagrees with the teachings found in the Bible. There is reason to suspect that future believers will be confronted with even stronger opposition from the unbelieving public. Therefore, it becomes even more important that we nurture the traits of tenacity, perseverance, and resilience, not only in ourselves, but in our children. If we lack these traits, the storms will blow our houses away, and we won't have the strength to rebuild.

> *Today mere inconvenience is equated with hardship.*

Endurance Training

Many great examples in scripture persisted in walking the walk of faith in spite of adversity, obstacles, or personal failures. We are the Lord's children, and He has us in training. We should have our own children and grandchildren in training to develop these traits. But these traits are best developed when life is not too easy.

In Hebrews 12:7 the writer identified trouble and adversity as a significant part of the Christian's training program when he said, "Endure hardship as discipline." Romans 5:3 then tells us what is accomplished during hard times: "We know that suffering produces perseverance"—the very trait that we all need in order to avoid becoming discouraged enough to quit. Further confirmation of this truth is found in James 1:3: "The testing of your faith develops perseverance."

In walking on a treadmill, I experienced the truth of this point. I noticed that the first ten minutes produced rather intense pain in my legs, but I learned that if I continued walking, in spite of the pain, I soon reached a point when the blood vessels expanded, and the pain subsided. If I had quit when I felt that early pain, I would never have achieved my goal. I would have thought that I had reached my personal limit in only ten minutes. Actually, it became easier to persevere because of the discipline to endure some pain for a little while.

All discipline involves some hardship, just as the writer of Hebrews 12:11 said, "It is not pleasant at the time, but painful." He encouraged us to strengthen our "feeble arms and weak knees" (Hebrews 12:12). We become stronger with each hurdle.

As parents, we are often tempted to want life to be easier for our children than it was for us. We might be wise to discipline *ourselves* to provide plenty of challenges and obstacles for our children and, therefore, train them never to quit. When children are given tasks, they should be trained to complete that task. Such discipline is neither pleasant for the parent or the child, but children are very blessed if they are taught that there are consequences for not completing goals.

> *We might be wise to discipline ourselves to provide plenty of challenges and obstacles for our children and, therefore, train them never to quit.*

Children also should learn the rewards for achieving goals. This kind of training develops tenacity and perseverance which will serve that child well all through life. Those are the very traits that will likely cause him to walk the Christian walk faithfully, without becoming discouraged enough to quit.

If holding fast and bouncing back after adversity is difficult for us, it's not too late to begin working hard to become more resilient. It's no accident that *perseverance* follows *self-control* in 2 Peter 1:6. Our resolve to endure, without giving up, will be tested repeatedly throughout life. It will require a *conscious decision* to struggle on through unpleasant circumstances without giving up. The more we exercise that kind of self-discipline, the more consistent the desired behavior becomes.

Resilience, tenacity, and perseverance are important, because they get us through the harshest times that life can deliver. Most important, a person with these characteristics is most likely remain faithful to the Lord. Many people quit the walk of faith, and that's the saddest of all failures.

When we read 2 Corinthians 11:23–26, we realize that the apostle Paul suffered unbelievable hardship and abuse. He mentioned that he was beaten by the Jews five times with thirty-nine lashes each time. He was almost killed several times. We are made to wonder what kind of person could continue to fight the fight of faith that Paul fought. What kind of person could continue to touch the lives of people who often didn't even appreciate his efforts?

> *"We know that suffering produces perseverance."*
> —ROMANS 5:3

It was a man who had become tenacious and resilient. He never considered giving up. He not only endured the tough times; he moved forward with an energetic spirit of zeal for the cause of Christ.

> *"We know that suffering produces perseverance."*
> Romans 5:3

*"But you are a chosen people,
a royal priesthood."*

———

1 PETER 2:9

Man given life sentence in fatal driveway holdup

He is to serve 40 years before parole eligibility

By Steve Scott
Staff-Writer of The Dallas Morning News

Derek Haggerty was sentenced Tuesday to life in prison for robbing and killing a retired banker in his Far North Dallas driveway last March.

Jurors in state District Judge Larry Baraka's court deliberated for two hours before convicting Mr. Haggerty of capital murder in the death of Robert C. "Bob" Scott.

Mr. Haggerty, 21, must serve at least 40 years before he is eligible for parole. He is the last of several defendants to be sent to prison in a string of similar robberies early last year.

Mr. Scott's wife, Pat Scott, embraced relatives and neighbors outside the courtroom. Among her supporters was Laura McManemin, whose husband, Michael, was killed by another driveway robber last year.

Ms. Scott, who recounted the robbery and killing for jurors last week, said Tuesday's verdict "makes me feel much safer."

She said she doesn't plan to leave the house she and her husband shared, even though the killing took place just outside.

"I'm staying," she said. "If they'd turned him loose, I might not have."

Mr. Haggerty's relatives declined to comment.

Mr. Scott, 63, was fatally shot March 3, 1994, by a man who robbed him and his wife shortly after they parked their car in their garage.

The robbery was one of a string of similar holdups by several groups of robbers in northern Dallas early last year. Mr. Haggerty was the last defendant to be tried in connection with those robberies.

The state's case against Mr. Haggerty included evidence that he bought the murder weapon several days before the killing and that he participated in pawning the Scotts' jewelry the day afterward.

Mr. Haggerty admitted buying the gun and pawning the Scotts' rings but testified that he was at a girlfriend's apartment at the time of the killing. The girlfriend told jurors that Mr. Haggerty had spent much of his time with her during the weeks surrounding the robbery but that she could not remember whether he was with her that day.

In closing arguments Tuesday, Assistant District Attorney Jason January attacked Mr. Haggerty's alibi, saying jurors should question why he never mentioned it in interviews with police.

"I guess he thinks 12 jurors are more gullible," Mr. January said.

He also reminded jurors of testimony from two women who identified Mr. Haggerty as the gunman who robbed them in their North Dallas driveways. Mr. January said similarities between those robberies and the one in which Mr. Scott was killed were too striking to ignore.

Defense attorney Charles Maduka said the state's evidence left plenty of room for doubt about Mr. Haggerty's guilt.

He pointed first to Ms. Scott's inability to identify Mr. Haggerty as her husband's killer.

"Does she have a reasonable doubt?" Mr. Maduka asked. "Should you have a reasonable doubt, if she does?"

Mr. Maduka also questioned the credibility of several of Mr. Haggerty's friends who testified against him. They did so, he said, in hopes of collecting reward money. Mr. Maduka also said jurors should discount testimony from several Dallas County jail inmates, who he said were "certified pathological liars."

One of the inmates testified that Mr. Haggerty admitted the killing to him.

CHAPTER

8

Remembering Who We Are

WHEN PEOPLE describe themselves, they often say, "I'm a teacher," or "I'm a spouse, a parent, a CPA, a technician, a physician, or a homemaker." If you suddenly could no longer say that you do that job, or you lost your family, *who* would you be then?

In the face of my life-changing tragedy, that question was one with which I wrestled. Those circumstances brought me more into focus about my identity than perhaps I had ever been. In a way, it was surprising that this identity question should perplex me, because apart from being a wife and mother, I had always had a rather fulfilling identity of my own. But the suddenness of the transition somehow shocked my senses into a clearer awareness that, now, I was someone different.

In a way that I had never before experienced, I began to absorb what our existence in this world is all about and that life is such a temporary thing. As is always the case when there has been a death, it was a time of going through possessions. During that time, those worldly goods seemed like meaningless dust-catchers, and I had the urge to just throw things away. I wondered, *Who would want this?* Those thoughts were distinctly tied to this new-found perspective that life is so fleeting, and possessions are so meaningless. Some people might consider such thinking to be depression, but I wasn't feeling depressed, just realistic. Even now that thinking was the clearest I have ever done about existence vs. eternity.

> *We are much more than this mortal existence, and we need to know it. What an uplifting realization! Great things await us.*

It's obvious that the writer of Psalms 39:5 agreed with my thoughts: "You have made my days a mere hand-breadth; the span of my years is nothing before you." He also wrote in Psalm 78:39, "He remembered that they were but flesh, a passing breeze that does not return."

Isaiah wrote in Isaiah 2:22, "Stop trusting in man who has but a breath in his nostrils."

Who Are We?

What more relevant mind-set can we have as we prepare for a day of adversity and trial than the knowledge of who we really are in God's scheme of things? Who are we really?

1. We are merely sojourners here on earth. The hymn that so clearly speaks this sentiment is *This World Is Not My Home.* One line of the song says, "I'm just passing through." Psalm 90:10 says, "The length of our days is seventy years— eighty if we have the strength." The national average for our life span is not much better than that today, even though some people are living longer. Psalm 103:15–16 says, "As for man his days are like grass, he flourishes like a flower of the field. The wind blows over it, and it is gone and its place remembers it no more."

People grace this earth a very short period of time. As we fill our spaces of time, we begin to think that the world could hardly get along without us. Yet, people die, and the world goes right on as if we had never been there, just like the flower spoken of by the psalmist.

Perhaps it would be beneficial for us to have a clearer awareness of who we are in God's big picture. We are much more than this mortal existence, and we need to know it. What an uplifting realization! Great things await us. Our Heavenly Father has promised us things too wonderful for our finite minds to imagine.

The Ultimate Tragedy

Still, our thinking becomes distorted as we live. Even though the road of life is sometimes bumpy, it's possible to enjoy the trip so much that our destination becomes completely irrelevant. People will go to almost any length to extend their stay here. Some people can't even bear to discuss the subject of departing this life. To most people, the ultimate tragedy is death, but death is not the ultimate tragedy. The ultimate tragedy is to make life's journey and fail to reach the promised land.

Something is very wrong with our thinking if this life is more desirable than heaven. Paul said in Philippians 1:23–24, "I desire to depart and be with Christ which is *better by far,* but it is more necessary for you that I remain in the body." Paul recognized that there is an existence that far exceeds what we presently experience here on this earth.

A friend once said, "Well, I want to go to heaven, but there are several places here on earth that I want to see first." It's so easy to forget who we are and go on living this life, hardly giving any thought to the special and wonderful place to which we are destined.

Some people—even Christians—feel that because of their earthly circumstances, they are *nobody*. Those people don't know who they are, because someone destined for heaven can hardly be considered a *nobody*.

2. We are chosen of God. In Romans 5:8, Paul writes, "While we were yet sinners, Christ died for us." In John 15:16, Jesus said, "You did not choose me, but I chose you." Later, to the church, Peter wrote, "But you are a chosen people, a royal priesthood" (1 Peter 2:9). When we become Christians, we move into a very special relationship with the Father, but even before we become Christians, we are important in God's eyes, because God has already chosen us. He is just waiting for *us* to choose *Him*.

Sometimes people can hardly comprehend that God views our souls as precious. It's awesome to think that Christ made that sacrifice for us long before we were born and hoped that we would choose to believe and obey. We may wonder, as David did, "What is man that you are mindful of him" (Psalm 8:4)? We might think that our God would have given up on us long ago, but the Bible has shown us that God sought us and bought us with the greatest sacrifice possible. With all our warts, we are His precious children. As we make the walk of faith, our Father coaxes us to be faithful.

> *Someone destined for heaven can hardly be considered a nobody.*

Does such knowledge mean anything to us in a time of adversity, disaster, and suffering? It certainly should! It should convict us that, no matter what the trouble, we don't struggle without a source of strength.

In John 14:16, Jesus told the disciples that they would not be left alone. He said, "I will ask the Father, and he will give you another comforter to be with you forever." The Greek word here for "comforter" means "someone who is called in to help or strengthen another person."

William Barclay, a Bible scholar, says, "We often talk of being able to cope with things. That is precisely the work of the Holy Spirit (comforter). He takes away our inadequacies and enables us to cope with life." This comforter is someone that each of us desperately needs in the trials of life.

> *We have been chosen by God, and because of our faith, we have the Holy Spirit living right inside us. We could hardly have it better!*

In Acts 2, when the church began, Peter preached, "Repent and be baptized every one of you, in the name of Jesus Christ so that your sins may be forgiven. And you will receive the gift of the Holy Spirit." Therefore, Christians have every reason to face adversity with great confidence, because we know who we are. We have been chosen by God, and because of our faith, we have the Holy Spirit living right inside us. We could hardly have it better!

3. Because of who we are, we need not live in fear. We live in a time when there are people who have little or no regard for human life. Our streets are often not safe, and fear of crime is a major concern in many of our communities. In the city of Dallas, Texas, many "gated communities" have sprung up since the crime took my husband's life. Unfortunately, people in Texas are now allowed to carry concealed weapons. So, fear is a common feeling.

It's sad that people have to be so fearful, but it's not a new phenomenon. There have been reasons to fear almost as long as people have lived. Most of us grew up reading stories or seeing movies about the early American settlers who lived in constant fear of attacks by hostile Indians. We can hardly imagine families living in such an unsafe environment, but we actually find ourselves living in similar high-risk conditions. God didn't promise that no tragedy or disaster would befall us, but He did promise to be with us through tragedy and disaster. Because of who we are, we can live without fear dominating our existence. Psalm 91:4 says this:

> *He will cover you with his feathers,*
> *and under his wings you will find refuge;*
> *his faithfulness will be your shield*
> *and rampart.*
> *You will not feel the terror of the night,*
> *nor the arrow that flies by day,*
> *nor the pestilence that stalks in the darkness,*
> *nor the plague that destroys at midday.*

Every night people turn on their security systems, slide their dead-bolts into place, and go to bed . . . hopefully, prepared. But in any great city, there are many who go to bed woefully *unprepared*, because they don't know God and, therefore, cannot put their confidence in Him. Still others, even though they have a relationship with God, have not yet learned to feel His guarding presence. A friend of mine, who has always lived alone, said that she has learned to lock her door and ask God to guard it. I, too, have been able to sleep without fear, and I give God the credit for being my refuge.

> *It doesn't do much good to be special if we don't know what privileges come with the package.*

It is urgent to know who we are and to hold fast to the privileges that are ours in Christ. It doesn't do much good to be special if we don't know what privileges come with the package.

I once heard a story about a gentleman who had saved his money for many years in order to take a cruise. When he purchased his ticket, he didn't have much money left over. He decided that he must be very frugal on this trip. One way he thought he might save money was to avoid going to the dining room. So, he spent the entire trip avoiding the meals. Toward the end of the trip, while conversing with a fellow traveler, he learned, to his dismay, that all the meals had been *included* in the price of the ticket. The poor man had missed one of the best parts of his cruise, because he didn't know what privileges came with the package.

People often miss many of the blessings of being a Christian, failing to grasp powerful advantages that are theirs through their relationship with the Father.

We commonly not only have fear, but we fear the wrong things. Jesus helps us to better understand when there is *reason* to fear with some very strong advice in Luke 12:4–7:

> I tell you, my friends, do not be afraid of those who kill the body and after that can do no more. But I tell you whom you should fear: Fear him who, after killing the body, has the power to throw you into hell. Yes, I tell you, fear him. Are not five sparrows sold for two pennies? Yet, not one of them is forgotten by God. Indeed, the very hairs of your head are numbered. Don't be afraid; you are worth more than any sparrows.

Who are you? You are someone special who doesn't need to live in fear, because there is much more than this life for you.

4. God will use our lives for His purposes. To understand this truth is to see ourselves and our lives in a new light.
We will view our lives as more purposeful, and the things that
happen in life will have more meaning. This perspective gives
us the incentive to struggle on through the disasters that befall
us, because we believe that God might be glorified, even in our
adversities.

Scripture assures us that bad things *will* happen to us. Personally, I view the bad things that happen as the work of Satan,
not God. It's Satan who wants to discourage our faith in God,
but God takes the evil that Satan brings to us and uses it for
our ultimate good. Often we don't even know what wondrous
ways God is glorified through our trials until they are over,
perhaps years down the road. And sometimes not at all. Even
so, He is still glorified.

In 2 Kings 5 a young slave girl was captured in Israel by
a band of soldiers and taken to Aram. How devastating it must
have been for her parents. Having lost their precious child,
naturally they viewed this situation as a disaster. They probably
never knew that the Lord used their daughter in a glorious way
when she referred Naaman to Elisha, the prophet of God, who
cleansed Naaman of leprosy.

To view our undesirable circumstances as something the
Lord can and will use gives us a sense that at least something
meaningful and positive can come from adversity. Often adversity appears senseless on the surface, but if we can remember
who we are and what God can do through us, we may gain a
new perspective from which to view the troubling circumstance.

The Attitude of Humility

The attitudes and perspectives we have contemplated in
this chapter are lofty goals indeed. However, there is yet another

aspect of knowing who we are that must not be overlooked—
the attitude of humility.

Jesus said of himself, "I am meek and lowly in heart . . ."
(Matthew 11:29, KJV). Learning to be secure enough about our
status as God's children should free us to serve others and to
do lowly tasks without accolades or thank yous.

If we really know who
we are, it frees us to become
better servants. The more secure we are about who we are,
the fewer ego problems we
have. If we are insecure in our
identities, we then worry
about our importance.

Some of the apostles felt
insecure about their own importance, and it caused them
to quarrel among themselves.
Contrast that egotistical atti-

> *The more secure we
> are about who we
> are, the fewer ego
> problems we have. If
> we are insecure in
> our identities, we
> then worry about
> our importance.*

tude of the apostles with the meek and lowly attitude of Jesus,
who was secure in who He was. Interestingly enough, in John
13:3, just before Jesus began washing the apostles' feet, there is
a sentence that emphasizes Jesus' awareness of who He was:
"Jesus knew that the Father had put all things under his power
and that he had come from God and was returning to God."
The passage then uses the conjunction "so," which is tanta-
mount to saying, "since Jesus knew who He was," He could
humble himself to perform the lowliest task. Even washing
dirty feet was not beneath His dignity. He didn't have to prove
to himself or to anyone else that He was God's own Son.

When we have to concern ourselves with our own status,
it can really handicap our ability to glorify God. It's embar-
rassing to admit that we are sometimes as guilty as the apostles

were of being prideful and causing disagreements over petty matters. Part of remembering who we are is to remember that we are as vulnerable as anyone else. Not one of us can get to heaven without the sacrifice of Jesus for our sins. As reassuring as it is to realize that we are God's own, we must humbly remember that we were bought with a price just like any other redeemed sinner.

> *While we bask in the assurance that we are children of the King, we must humbly acknowledge that we hold that status only by the grace of God.*

When we see people who don't know or acknowledge Christ, and they are living a deplorable life, we should never forget that we, too, are frail and would be just as lost without the sacrifice of Jesus. Jesus directed one of His parables "to some who were confident in their own righteousness and looked down on everyone else." In Luke 18:9–14, Jesus said,

> Two men went up to the temple to pray, one a Pharisee and the other a tax collector. The Pharisee stood up and prayed about himself: "God, I thank you that I am not like all other men—robbers, evildoers, adulterers—or even this tax collector. I fast twice a week and give a tenth of all I get." But the tax collector stood at a distance. He would not even look up to heaven, but beat his breast and said, "God, have mercy on me, a sinner." I tell you that this man, rather than the other, went home justified before God. For everyone who exalts himself will be humbled, and he who humbles himself will be exalted.

While we bask in the assurance that we are children of the King, we must humbly acknowledge that we hold that status only by the grace of God.

A Look in the Mirror

In his book *Psycho-Cybernetics,* Dr. Maxwell Maltz says that everyone carries a mental picture of himself. It may be ill-defined, but it is there! Dr. Maltz contends that we have our own beliefs about ourselves and that these beliefs are based on past experiences, such as successes and failures or how other people have always responded to us. He says that we tend to act out who we perceive ourselves to be. If Dr. Maltz's premise is correct, and there is obviously much truth in his statements, then many people will be in deep trouble

> *It's not possible for us to think positively about our circumstances if we think negatively about ourselves.*

emotionally when serious adversity strikes. It's not possible for us to think positively about our circumstances if we think negatively about ourselves.

It is possible, however, for us to remake our self-images at any stage of life. This change can come about when we learn who God is! Even with a poor self-image, for all the reasons that Dr. Maltz mentioned, we may at some stage get a new lease on life. Suddenly, we can become someone of worth, because God says that is who *He* is. We can, quite literally, become new people.

Unfortunately, there are others who go through the prescribed motions of becoming God's child but never quite understand how special and loved they are by God. They continue to view Him as some stern and distant ruler. Such a view does not allow them to be built up by God's great love and closeness.

The scriptures overflow with examples of people who had every reason to feel unworthy of God's love because of their past lives. The apostle Peter said to Jesus in Luke 5:8, "Go away from me, Lord; I am a sinful man!" He later wrote to Christians in 1 Peter 4:3, "You have spent enough time in the past doing what pagans choose to do—living in debauchery, lust, drunkenness, orgies, carousing, and detestable idolatry." Our pasts don't make us second-class citizens in the Lord's kingdom. God has put the sinner's past from His mind, and He desires that Christians *renew* our own minds (2 Corinthians 4:16). Only the "renewed mind" will be able to draw really near to God.

> *Our pasts don't make us second-class citizens in the Lord's kingdom.*

In order for us to feel good about who we are, we must feel loved. Some psychologists say that to have felt loved only *once* is not enough to satisfy our need. The feeling of being loved is something that has to be replenished on a regular basis. A wife needs her husband to tell her, or show her, his love regularly, and the husband has the same need. This is also true in the parent/child relationship.

Christians are loved by God and are special people because of that love. Even in this special relationship, though, we need to be reminded regularly of the powerful love of God in order to remember who we are. How can we be reminded regularly of God's love?

Alone with God

In the church where I worship, the minister recently preached a series of sermons about learning to be quiet and alone with God. In our frenzied society, we feel guilty if we aren't juggling several activities simultaneously. Then, when someone asks us, "What have you been doing, lately?" we can hardly think of anything worth mentioning. So, what do we do that crowds God out of our lives? Can we not block out some time to be alone with God and reflect on who we are supposed to be?

Jesus found it necessary to withdraw from the crowds to pray and draw near to God. That kept Him centered on who He was and that God was working His purpose through Him. Do we need that reminder less than Jesus did? If we don't regularly spend time quietly reflecting on God's Word, the assurance of God's love will fade from our hearts. His Word repeatedly tells us of His love; it is His way of speaking to us. There is no way that we can put the adversity of this life in proper perspective without an ongoing relationship with God and without being reminded that heaven is our destination. Without that reminder, we become concerned with affairs of this life and forget who we really are.

I Am Who I Am

If someone had asked me a few years ago to write a paragraph, describing who I was, I probably would have said, "I am a wife, a mother, an elder's wife, a banker's wife, etc." Then I was no longer a banker's wife nor an elder's wife. In fact, I was not even a wife. So, who was I?

In reality, I was who I had always been, but it had not even been on my list. I was God's chosen child, His loved one— descriptions that can never be taken away. That's who I will always be, no matter what disaster comes. That's also who *you* can be.

Realizing that I had always been God's person helped me to realize that I could just continue to be that same person. It gave me a sense of direction and continuity for my life, even though so much had changed. Therefore, I would continue to serve the Lord in whatever capacity that He saw fit to use me.

About six months after Bob's death, I began a grief recovery group for women. About that same time, I resumed my speaking engagements. There's little time to wonder who I am these days, but if anyone asks, I will be able to tell them, "I am who I am." And that's because I know the God who has helped me batten down the hatches and weather the storms of life.

Then we cried out to the Lord
in our trouble,
and he brought us out of our distress.
He stilled the storm to a whisper;
the waves of the sea were hushed.
We were glad when it grew calm,
and he guided us to our
desired haven.
Let us give thanks to the Lord
for his unfailing love
and his wonderful deeds for us.
Let us exalt him in the
assembly of the people
and praise him in the council
of the elders.

———

PSALM 107:28–32, ADAPTED

Epilogue

THE TRIAL for Derek Haggerty, the man accused of murdering my husband, began on February 27, 1995, following two postponements. I had dreaded and feared the prospect of testifying before a courtroom filled with people. The thought of hearing our entire ordeal dissected in such a public forum made me feel ill, but I desperately wanted it finished.

I was not allowed to be in the courtroom until after I testified. The rest of my family and friends were in the courtroom to hear all of the testimony. On the third day of the trial, I was brought down from the District Attorney's office and sworn in to testify. I kept thinking, *This can't be real!* I couldn't have been more nervous if I had been the defendant myself.

For the first time, I sat looking into the eyes of my attacker and my husband's murderer. His face was full of hostility and contempt, but I just sat there for a moment looking at him. I was actually devoid of feeling about this man—no vengeance, not even any anger.

After I had finished testifying, I was allowed to sit in the courtroom with my family. It was stressful to hear all the witnesses, but I wanted to be there. Eventually, the defendant insisted on testifying himself. His arrogance did not serve him well.

There was a tremendous amount of evidence against the defendant. He was positively identified by two other driveway robbery victims as being their attacker. When he was arrested, the murder weapon had been in his pickup truck, and the gun clip had been in his pocket. The pawnshop employees to whom he sold our jewelry also identified him.

The anniversary of Bob's death came and went during the trial. And, ironically, on Tuesday, March 7, 1995, exactly one year from the day of Bob's funeral, the defendant was found guilty and sentenced to life in prison. Under Texas law that means that he must serve forty years before being eligible for parole.

A few months after the trial, he was tried for another driveway robbery and was sentenced to twenty-five years to be served consecutively. So, Derek Haggerty is currently serving a sixty-five-year sentence.

He has now appealed our case on the grounds of inadequate counsel, and his parents have hired a new attorney.

What will happen in coming days and months? I don't know. But I do know who will be with me during it all, and He is more than able to see me through the storm.

Leader's Guide

TO THE LEADER:

The following discussion thoughts and questions on each of the eight chapters in this book have been provided to help you and your study group gain as much insight and instruction as possible from this excellent study by Pat Scott. May God bless you as you learn together to *Batten Down the Hatches* and prepare for the storms of life.

CHAPTER 1

1. Read this chapter and try to imagine yourself in Pat's place.

2. Discuss 1 Corinthians 15:55 and how it relates to this chapter.

3. Discuss how this verse relates to members of the class and their own life storms, either past or present.

4. Close this session with a prayer for God's constant presence throughout the storms of life.

CHAPTER 2

1. Why do people tend to resist change?

2. What hinders people from planning for and discussing changes that can be expected?

3. What are some things that we might do in order to prepare for expected changes?

4. If your life suddenly changed irreversibly, what might help you to accept the fact that your life would never be the same again? Discuss.

5. Discuss Paul's formula for accepting change. What is your goal?

6. Share your perspective about the problems and pain in this life versus your ultimate goal.

7. Discuss the significance of I Thessalonians 5:18 as it applies to difficult times.

8. When you experience significant loss, what can stay the same about your life?

9. Do you think that you will remember this life's adversity in heaven? Why?

10. What are the advantages of learning and experiencing new things?

CHAPTER 3

1. When you experience setbacks or difficulties, do you tend to consider them permanent or temporary?

2. Have you ever experienced something that seemed disastrous but later derived blessings from it?

3. Share experiences of difficult times when God supplied just what was needed.

4. List some by-products of having a positive and optimistic outlook.

5. Is it possible to improve our outlook on life? What are the implications of Philippians 4:8–9?

6. Which do you notice more readily about your children, your spouse, or your friends—their good points or their flaws?

7. Are negative thoughts about people harmless as long as they are private? Will those thoughts affect who *you* are?

8. Have you noticed that what you focus on expands? Share some techniques for punching the reset button.

9. Read and discuss the message of Psalms 37:1–11.

CHAPTER 4

1. Discuss the implications of 2 Corinthians 12:9.

2. Share with the group some everyday victories you have enjoyed.

3. Discuss the specific role that knowledge plays in learning to trust God. What role does faith play? How do these two factors harmonize? Discuss Romans 10:2 and Romans 10:17.

4. Discuss David's view of God's role in his life. Can we acquire that closeness to God?

5. Is your faith dependent upon understanding why bad things happen in your life? If you knew *why* bad things happen, what would it change?

6. Do you think that you could view God as your refuge and shelter if you were confronted with a major personal tragedy? Would you blame God or Satan?

7. What significance do you attach to 1 Peter 5:8?

8. In scripture our relationship with God is portrayed in several different ways—our creator, our father, our judge, our disciplinarian. When you experience bad times, in what role do you view God?

9. Are we in a position to judge God's fairness? Explain.

CHAPTER 5

1. Can you think of an instance when Jesus declined to help someone because He was busy with something else?

2. Do opportunities to help others come when you are already overloaded? What should be our response in such a situation?

3. Are you more like the Good Samaritan or the priest and Levite? Discuss today's considerations in similar situations. Is it more dangerous today to help people?

4. Can the Spirit be alive and well in us if we don't care about other people? Discuss.

5. Do you believe that God supplies our opportunities to serve?

6. Discuss the implications of 2 Corinthians 1:4.

7. Discuss ways that caring for the wounded prepares us for our own adversity.

8. Do you believe that the wounded see Jesus in those who help them? Discuss.

9. Is it possible that Christians are selective in their outreach today? Why?

CHAPTER 6

1. Which do you believe is more difficult to control—the tongue or the thought process?

2. Do you practice controlling the way you think about affairs of this world in light of eternity? Could this manner of thinking benefit you in a time of adversity?

3. Review and discuss the variance in meaning of the Greek words translated as "self-control" used in Galatians 5:23 and 2 Peter 1:13.

4. Do you believe that someone who has never practiced self-control can develop it?

5. Emotional and unwise choices are normal occurrences in the face of calamity. Discuss the possible role of self-control in such situations.

6. Review some of the things that God said to Job in chapters 38–41 of that book.

7. What are some specific areas of life today in which people have difficulty practicing self-control?

8. Share some ideas for learning to practice better self-control in preparation for a future day of adversity.

9. Why is it so necessary to move beyond irrational thinking after a crisis or tragedy?

CHAPTER 7

1. What is there about experiencing adversity that better enables us to be used for God's purposes?

2. Do you believe that quitting in the midst of adversity is a *conscious* decision? Discuss.

3. What was God's prescription for strengthening Elijah's will to go on? Have you known of instances of discouragement similar to Elijah's in 1 Kings 19:5–8? Describe.

5. Discuss how God works His purposes through us today.

6. In what ways are traits like tenacity and perseverance developed? (Refer to Romans 5:3 and James 1:3.)